CHANGE HAPPENS

CHANGE HAPPENS

When to Try Harder
and When to Stop Trying So Hard

Avrum Geurin Weiss

ROWMAN & LITTLEFIELD PUBLISHERS, INC.
Lanham • Boulder • New York • Toronto • Plymouth, UK

Published by Rowman & Littlefield Publishers, Inc.
A wholly owned subsidary of The Rowman & Littlefield Publishing Group, Inc.
4501 Forbes Boulevard, Suite 200, Lanham, Maryland 20706
http://www.rowmanlittlefield.com

Estover Road, Plymouth PL6 7PY, United Kingdom

British Library Cataloguing in Publication Information Available

Library of Congress Cataloging-in-Publication Data

Weiss, Avrum Geurin.
 Change happens : when to try harder and when to stop trying so hard /
Avrum Weiss.
 p. cm.
"Published in partnership with the American Educational Research
Association."
 ISBN 978-1-4422-1149-0 (cloth : alk. paper) — ISBN 978-1-4422-1151-3
(electronic)
 1. Change (Psychology). 2. Interpersonal relations. I. Title.
 BF637.C4W447 2011
 158—dc23   2011021360

Printed in the United States of America

For Sarra, my precious daughter

TABLE OF CONTENTS

ACKNOWLEDGMENTS

I would like to thank:

My closest friend, Robert Carrere, Ph.D., and my sister, Rachel Weiss, both extraordinary authors in their own right, who never faltered in their belief in this project.

Gayanne, for her patience and support through the many highs and lows.

Debbara Dingman, Ph.D., my fabulous cotherapist who helped me to formulate many of the ideas for this book and put up with me through so many years of rejections and heartache.

Roni Cohen-Sandler, Ph.D., who generously took me under her wing and guided me through all of the vicissitudes of bringing this project to fruition.

Loretta Barrett, who read countless early versions of this book and spent many hours trying to help me organize these complex ideas into a marketable product.

Andy Ross, my fabulous agent who never stopped believing in this project.

Linda Bryant, cofounder of Charis Books in Atlanta who helped me realize I wanted to write this book for a general audience.

Harville Hendrix, Ph.D., an early reader and supporter.

Lyn Somer, Ph.D., one of my first readers who gave me the gift of telling me how these ideas helped her change her life, and then introduced me to a long string of friends and colleagues who all gave so generously of their time and support.

My colleagues in my AAP "family group" who have loved me and supported me more than I could have ever imagined, and helped me get over my fear of success: Fern Beu, Ph.D., Damon Blank, M.Ed, Frances Compton, Ph.D., Debbara Dingman, Ph.D., Marc Feldman, Ph.D., Gary Frankel, Ph.D., Doris Jackson, Ph.D., Laurie Michaels, Ph.D., Robert Rosenblatt, Ph.D., Reginald Schoonover, Ph.D., Lyn Somer, Ph.D., and Kathryn Van der Heiden, MS.

My partners in practice at Pine River Psychotherapy Associates who have encouraged me to be my best self as a person and as a psychotherapist: Nancy Cooley, Ph.D., Robert Coyle, Ph.D., Debbara Dingman, Ph.D., Ruth Hepler, Ph.D., Marlyne Israelian, Ph.D., Bernhard Kempler, Ph.D., Luis McLeod, Ph.D., Ndiya Nkongho, Ph.D., Bruce Pemberton, Ed.D., Judy Pemberton, Ph.D., and Mark Timberlake, Ph.D.

FROG AND TOAD: THE GARDEN

In the classic children's series *Frog and Toad* there is a story called *The Garden*[1] in which Toad asks Frog to teach him how to grow a garden. Frog gives Toad some seeds, tells him to plant them in the ground, and he will soon have a garden.

Toad went home and planted the seeds, but he got impatient because the seeds did not come up right away. Toad talked to his seeds, sang to his seeds, he even yelled at his seeds, but still they still did not grow. Frog told Toad that his seeds were not coming up because he had scared them and if he would just leave them alone for a few days, the seeds would grow.

A few days later, when his seeds still had not come up, Toad decided the problem was that his seeds were afraid of the dark, so he sat outside all night in his garden with lighted candles and read stories to his seeds. Then Toad fell asleep. The next morning Frog came by and woke Toad, pointing out that little green plants were coming up out of the ground.

Toad was ecstatic, but exhausted, saying, "You were right, Frog. It was very hard work."[2]

PREFACE

Whatever authority I may have rests solely on knowing how little
I know.

—Socrates[1]

I do not sit down at my desk to put into verse something that is already clear in my mind. If it were clear in my mind, I should have
no incentive or need to write about it. . . . We do not write in order
to be understood; we write in order to understand.

—C. Day Lewis[2]

Human experience has always fascinated me. Like most therapists, I
went into the field initially to better understand my own family and get
help for myself. I remember walking down the street as a young man and
mimicking the way people held their bodies or the expression on their
faces, just to see what it might feel like to be them. Occasionally a patient
asks me, "Don't you get bored sitting and listening to people talk about
their problems all day long?" Of course I get bored sometimes, but only
when I am not really listening. Just when I start to think I have heard it
all, someone tells me something about how he lives or how she sees the
world that truly amazes me. I was bound to become a psychologist.

I have always been interested in the big questions in psychology, the questions we tend to skip over and act as if we have thoroughly explored. For example, my early research was on the patient's experience of privacy in psychotherapy, because most research is about the value of self-disclosure and we don't talk as much about the importance of discretion, about learning how to make ongoing relational decisions about what to disclose, to whom and when.[3]

The process of change is one of those large questions we have largely neglected. There is a good deal of research on techniques to help people change and methods to measure change, but we have not been nearly as thoughtful about the actual *experience* of change. We also tend to be more oriented toward pathology than wellness, so we know more about why people do not change than about what happens when they do. Few therapists have any graduate-level training that addresses the process of change in psychotherapy, and have rarely thought through their own theory of how people change.[4] How can a field dedicated to helping people change be so unreflective about the experience of change?

While we are not very reflective about the process of change, as a culture we are obsessed with change. The pace of our lives keeps moving faster and faster. Like sharks, we seem to believe our vitality depends on constant motion. We are inundated with advertising telling us we can only be happy by changing who we are: by looking younger or thinner, consuming more, or perfectly executing all of the overlapping roles of our lives.

Some of the most important areas of our lives that we used to rely on for constancy and stability are now filled with flux. The average American moves once every seven years.[5] Between forty and sixty percent of new marriages will eventually end in divorce, and only about twenty-five percent of children in this country grow up in an intact nuclear family.[6] The security of a lifelong career with one company has become almost unheard of, and we are becoming increasingly isolated as our traditional communities disappear.

Like any good researcher, I began by reflecting on my own experiences of change. I noticed that I have two very different experiences of change. Sometimes I am able to make significant changes in my life by hanging in there and Trying Harder. For example, my father was a very angry man and when I first became a father, I had to work to keep a check on my anger. Initially, it took my full attention to stay on top of my anger. Gradually, over a period of years, it got progressively easier and more natural for me. People now often comment on how calm I am and how hard it is for them to imagine me being angry, but it is still difficult for me to see myself that way.

On the other hand, sometimes I just cannot make any headway with what I am trying to change, no matter how hard I try. For example, for many years I struggled to be financially responsible. Even when I had young children, I did not have disability insurance or a will. I just could not take care of these normal adult tasks no matter how hard I tried. Some years later, shortly after my mother's death, I realized that I had purchased disability insurance and executed a will without even thinking about it. Paradoxically, it seemed as if I was able to make this important change only after I Stopped Trying So Hard to change.

I also started paying much closer attention to how my patients changed, and I invited them to talk with me more about their experience of change. I found that my patients' experiences paralleled my own; sometimes they were only able to change by Trying Harder, and other times they changed only after they Stopped Trying So Hard.

Next, I reviewed theories of change in the professional literature, and found descriptions of the same two broad approaches to change. Some psychological theorists talk about change as a conscious process of Trying Harder while others argue that change is primarily unconscious and requires letting go of consciously trying so hard. Most of my training provided indoctrination in the self-righteous certainty of Stop Trying So Hard approaches to change, and I excelled in clever theoretical critiques of Trying Harder approaches. However, middle age and the wisdom of my patients gradually robbed me of this and many other false certainties. The simple question of "which approach is better?" was replaced with two more helpful questions: "What underlying factors do these two approaches share that makes them both effective?" and "How can I learn how to integrate these two approaches most effectively to help my patients?"

As I pursued these new questions, I noticed a real shift in my work as a therapist. I first noticed this shift with a number of patients who had long-standing but unacknowledged problems with alcohol. A number of patients in my practice started to pay attention to their alcohol use in ways that started ripples of profound change though every aspect of their lives. For many years, I thought that people sometimes change over the course of psychotherapy and sometimes did not. As I continued to learn more about the underlying factors that facilitate change across all settings, I began to think of change as the natural, almost inevitable outcome of the therapeutic process.

Many of you are reading this book because there is something you want to change about your life. Some of you are reading this book primarily to learn more about helping other people change, but of course the best way to help others change is to learn more about changing yourself. *Change Happens* can help you with these and other life changes. *Change Happens* is designed as a companion to other self-help books, a guide that will help you to make better use of the information and strategies contained in other self-help books that address more specific life issues. If you have not yet started the change you want to create in your life, then *Change Happens* will help you figure out the most effective way to begin that change. If you have already tried other approaches to change and been unsuccessful, *Change Happens* will help you understand what went wrong without blaming yourself, and help you learn how to increase your chances of success by knowing when to Try Harder and when to Stop Trying So Hard.

Learning how to change your life is like learning how to cook a great meal. You eat a great meal at a friend's house and you want to be able to make the same meal, so you ask your friend for the recipe. Some people are disappointed when the cook tells them, "Add a dash of this" or "Season to taste" or "Simmer until it looks done." They are worried that they won't know how much to add or how long to cook it, and that it won't turn out right if they add too much or too little, or cook it too long or not long enough. They hoped for something more like "Add ¼ teaspoon of this" or "Cook 12½ minutes at low heat." Recipes are often not that precise because every cook and every kitchen are just a little bit different, so adjustments have to be made for every situation. This book has recipes for changing your life, but they are broad recipes about the process of change in general. You will have to adapt these recipes to the specifics of who you are and how you live your life.

The primary premise of *Change Happens* is that embracing experience is the key to change. The more fully we embrace our experience the more we change, and the more disconnected we become from our experience the less we change. Accordingly, the more fully you embrace your experience in reading this book, the more you will change.

Let me suggest that you approach this book like a sumptuous seven-course gourmet feast. Take your time and savor any part that speaks particularly to you. Try to allow reading this book to enter your experience at all levels, conscious and unconscious. Consider the possibility that the ideas that you are currently holding onto about change are actually a part of what is preventing you from changing. Consider that somewhere inside you may already know everything you need to know about change, but that you have been unable to access it.

The purpose of this book is not to convince you that either Trying Harder or Not Trying So Hard is a better approach, but to help you be more comfortable integrating both of these approaches. People get stuck not because they start with the wrong approach to change; they get stuck when they don't make the appropriate adjustments along the way. Effective and enduring change depends on knowing *when* to Try Harder and *when* to Stop Trying So Hard.

EXERCISE

Before you read any further, I would like to invite you to set this book aside, and reflect about your own experience of change. Find a quiet space where you can count on being uninterrupted for a while, and bring something with you to record your thoughts. Write a description of one or more significant experiences of change in your life. Write about whatever experiences come to mind. You can write about a big change like recovering from an illness or falling in love, or a more specific change like getting a promotion or overcoming a particular fear. You can write about a discrete event, like starting a new exercise program or about a process that unfolded over time, like becoming more loving and less critical toward your family. Just choose something that feels important to you.

Begin at whatever seems like the natural starting place, and walk through the entire experience in as much detail as you can. Write about your experience as you actually lived it, rather than your thoughts or analysis of your experience. Write in the first person, from the inside-out, rather than from the outside looking in at yourself. Write about what you saw, what you felt, what you thought, what you smelled and tasted. Tell the story so that someone reading it can get a sense of what it was like to be you during that experience.

When you are finished, take your description of change and tuck it inside the cover of this book. As you read, pull out your description of change from time to time and use your own experience to help you judge what is most helpful and what is less helpful to you as you read this book. Buddha said, "Believe nothing, no matter where you read it or who has said it, not even if I have said it, unless it agrees with your own common sense." Thus, we encounter the first of many paradoxes. I have just offered you an external suggestion to value your own internal experience above external suggestions. You will find many more such paradoxes as we walk together on the path of change. I wish you bon voyage on your journey.

A note on language usage: You may notice that I use the term *patient* rather than the more currently popular *client*. The term *client* is derived from the Latin "cliens," meaning a freed slave who retains an economic dependency on his former master.[7] It describes a business relationship, an exchange of fee-for-service. The term *patient* suggests a relationship whose focus is healing. It implies a giving over to a process that is bigger and more powerful than we are. To allow ourselves to become a patient is to let go of the psychological status quo that has failed us some time ago to consider the frightening possibility that we do not understand everything that is going on, and may not be able to get where we want to go without help. I am a client to my accountant. I prefer to be a patient to my psychotherapist.

1

TWO WAYS TO CHANGE

The opposite of a fact is falsehood, but the opposite of one profound truth may very well be another profound truth.

—Niels Bohr[1]

You want to change something about your life. It may be a relatively small and straightforward change; perhaps you would like to spend a little more time with your family, get to the gym more consistently, or be more productive at work. Or you may be considering a larger change. Perhaps you feel lonely and want to expand your network of friends or deepen the intimacy you share with loved ones. Maybe you have not quite lived up to some of your own hopes and expectations and you want to find the courage to live more of the life you secretly dream of: quit the job you have never liked and pursue the work you love or leave a loveless marriage and face your own fears of being alone. It may even be that your life feels out of control in some ways, and you swing wildly back and forth between a resigned sense of detachment and a rising feeling of urgency whenever you allow yourself to think about where your life is headed. You want to make this change in your life and you are committed to doing whatever it takes to be successful.

WHAT KIND OF CHANGE?

When I was young and free and my imagination had no limits, I dreamed of changing the world. As I grew older and wiser, I discovered the world would not change, so I shortened my sights somewhat and decided to change only my country.

But it, too, seemed immovable.

As I grew into my twilight years, in one last desperate attempt, I settled for changing only my family, those closest to me, but alas, they would have none of it.

And now as I lie on my deathbed, I suddenly realize: If I had only changed my self first, then by example I would have changed my family.

From their inspiration and encouragement, I would then have been able to better my country and, who knows, I may have even changed the world.

—From the tomb of an Anglican bishop in the crypts of Westminster Abbey

We can think about two kinds of change: external and internal change. External change is the kind of change that you and everyone around you can see. External change is reassuring because you can see it and sometimes even measure it, and even if you do not recognize that change in yourself, other people can see it and point it out to you. Internal change involves shifts in your subjective experience: changes in the way you feel, think, and perceive that may or may not be visible to others. Internal change can be more subtle and difficult for you and those around you to notice.

In this culture, we tend to focus more on external change. In a national survey that asked what people would change to make their lives happier, thirty-three percent said they would change their financial situation and fourteen percent said they would change their job. Nine percent of people said they would change where they live, five percent said their appearance, five percent their family, five percent would change their romantic situation, and four percent said they would change their health. Notice that the first two priorities are both about money, and external changes account for over sixty percent of the change that people want to create in their lives, whereas internal change accounted for less than fifteen percent of what people wanted to change (C. W. Brown, personal communication, 2008).

However, if you listen closely to people when they talk about the external change they want to create in their lives you will often hear the internal change that goes along with it. When people talk about wanting to be more assertive, you may also hear them talking about learning to feel stronger internally, less intimidated and less easily knocked off center. When people talk about wanting to live within their means or eat more healthily, you may also hear them talk about wanting to learn how to be more self-loving, or feel less internally out of control. When people talk about wanting to find a life partner, if you listen carefully, you may hear them talk about wanting to feel less internally alone.

In *Change Happens,* we are going to talk about both external and internal change, about changes in both your subjective experience and the ways in which you act in the world and the relationship between the two.

DO PEOPLE REALLY CHANGE?

> The one unchangeable certainty is that nothing is certain or unchangeable.
> —John Fitzgerald Kennedy[2]

The question is often asked whether we ever change who we truly are, or just learn how to adapt to different circumstances. It is a critically important question because if change is nothing more then adaptation, then you cannot count on it in yourself or in others. If my partner changes her behavior only because I stopped talking to her, I am not very confident that change will endure when I start being nice to her again. On the other hand, if my partner has truly changed because something has shifted inside her and she recognizes how her behavior was affecting me, then I might be able to relax into this change.

We know that people do make substantial changes in their lives every day, from the ordinary to the dramatic; from scheduling a long-delayed physical to surviving cancer, from learning how to live within their means to turning around the fortunes of a failing business, from revitalizing their sexual relationship to leaving an abusive marriage. Researchers estimate that forty percent of people recover on their own from even some of the most stubborn, difficult-to-treat psychological problems like alcoholism, borderline personality disorder, and antisocial personality disorder.[3]

On the other hand, some life changes can seem inexplicably difficult to make, and maddeningly challenging to maintain. For example, although about half of the people in this country make a New Year's resolution, only fifty-five percent are able to sustain the resolution for two weeks, and the number is down to nineteen percent after two years.[4] More dramatically, about 600,000 people have coronary bypasses every year in the United States, but two years after surgery, only ten percent of those patients maintain the lifestyle change necessary to help keep them alive.[5] Despite how difficult it can be to make and sustain important life changes, we hang in there, determined to change even in the face of sometimes-daunting odds. The average person makes the same New Year's resolution ten years running, each year rationalizing their past failures to convince themselves to try, try again.[6]

How can we make sense of this apparent contradiction? How is it possible for us to be able to make substantial, often life-altering changes, sometimes against great odds, when other times we struggle with the simplest changes, even when our very lives may depend on it? The answer is that we all have within us a critical balance between our need for novelty and change, known as *neophilia,* and our needs for stability, known as *neophobia.*

On one hand, human beings are particularly well equipped for change. We are born with fewer innate instincts than other species, and we have an extended developmental period, creating more opportunities for ongoing change through adapting to our environment. Humans also have a far more developed sense of inquisitiveness and curiosity about our environments that extends into adult development, and our ability to learn through imitation rather than simple trial-and-error learning is also far more advanced.[7]

Our success as a species, however, is not attributable just to our advanced capacity for change, but to our ability to strike an exquisite balance between neophilia and neophobia, a balance between our capacity to change and adapt to our environment and our ability to maintain stability in the face of a rapidly changing environment. We are capable of both dramatic change in the face of daunting obstacles, and impressive stability in the face of chaotic circumstances.

TWO WAYS TO CHANGE

I own an old twenty-six-foot sailboat that I keep on the coast of Georgia. One day I was sailing near Savannah, about three miles off shore, just following the wind, out there for the pure joy of sailing rather than heading toward any particular destination. I was sailing east on a beam reach, with the wind coming from the north, making a comfortable five to six knots. To sail upwind I had to first push the tiller away from me to change course, and then hold the tiller steady against the force of the fifteen-knot wind. The wind was in my face now and the boat heeled over. It was exhilarating but it was hard work. To sail downwind all I had to do was release the tiller and let the boat follow the wind. Now the wind was behind me and the boat sailed without heel. It was not nearly as exciting, but it was a lot less work.

Similarly, there are two broad approaches to changing the course of your life. If you browse the self-help section of your local bookstore, you will find a variety of books suggesting you can change your life simply by Trying Harder. Trying Harder is about taking action and changing from the outside in, changing how we act or changing the external circumstances of our lives in order to change ourselves.

One summer I went to an amusement park with my extended family. My sister was very frightened of the big roller coaster, but she was determined to overcome her fear. We rode the roller coaster together, and she was petrified as soon as the cars began to move. She clutched my arm fiercely and cried through the whole ride. Towards the end of the same day, several of us decided to ride that same roller coaster again. My sister, in a classic example of outside-in change, decided to force herself back onto that ride in order to overcome her fear. I have a picture of her at the top of the biggest hill with an ear-to-ear grin on her face.

Whether it is dating, dieting, or dealing with a job crisis, we like to believe we can change just about anything if we are only willing to work hard enough. As the Nike ads suggest, "Just do it." Trying Harder is a simple, conscious model that reduces change to the process of setting clear goals and objectives. An article in a popular women's magazine advised readers, "Without goals you remain what you were: With goals you become what you wish."[8]

If you move over to the spirituality section of the same bookstore, you will find books offering the opposite advice. These books suggest being committed to Trying Harder is part of what prevents us from changing, and we have to Stop Trying So Hard in order to change our lives. Not Trying So Hard is about changing from the inside out, accepting ourselves internally in order to change how we act or change the external circumstances of our lives. Had my sister decided to use an inside-out approach to dealing with her fear she might have found a quiet place to sit and do some deep muscle relaxation or yoga breathing, or sat and talked with someone to try to calm herself before attempting the roller coaster again. Not Trying So Hard is a relatively complex unconscious model that equates change with being rather than doing. Prayer, psychotherapy, and meditation are all examples of change through Not Trying So Hard.

In the biblical story of Exodus, as the Egyptians converged on the children of Israel standing on the shores of the Red Sea, God instructed Moses to tell the people to Stop Trying So Hard and have the faith to "stand firm . . . you only need to be still."[9] The Rabbis, however, add an additional commentary, called a *midrash,* to the story. In the Rabbi's story another man named Nachshon showed a different kind of faith by Trying Harder, moving forward, and wading into the waters before they parted.

Table 1.1 is a summary of some of the characteristics of Trying Harder and Not Trying So Hard.

Now let us look at Table 1.2 for some specific life issues people often want to change, and see how they look when approached by Trying Harder or by Not Trying So Hard.

Do you recognize yourself in this table? Do the Trying Harder or the Not Trying So Hard strategies seem more familiar or make more sense to you? You may have noticed that both columns made a lot of sense. You have probably used techniques from both columns successfully yourself. Everyone has advice, solicited and unsolicited, about the best way to change your life, from friends and family to self-help books, television talk shows, and magazines. People can be surprisingly adamant about how they think you should go about changing your life; sometimes they are even offended if you do not do it the way they recommend. The problem is this fervent advice from friends and loved ones is more about what has been helpful for them, which may not be what will work best for you.

Table 1.1

Trying Harder	Not Trying So Hard
Change is Outside In: If change equals the distance between the way things are and the way you expect them to be, then the most effective path to happiness is to change the way things are, change how you behave, or change the external circumstances of your life in order to change who you are internally.	Change is Inside Out: If change equals the distance between the way things are and the way you expect them to be, then the most effective path to happiness is to change yourself, change who you are internally in order to change how you behave, or change the external circumstances of your life.
Change is conscious: We are capable of consciously knowing just what we need to change in order to be happier in our lives.	Change is unconscious: What we unconsciously want generally outweighs our conscious desires.
Change requires a plan: Once you have figured out what you want to change, the best way to get there is to formulate a step-by-step plan with clear goals and objectives.	Plans can interfere with change: Sometimes our insistence on having a plan can interfere with the natural unfolding of the process of change.
Change is about what you do, it requires action: Change is about doing. It requires formulating a specific plan of action. Sitting there passively and just wanting to change won't make it happen.	Change is about who you are. It requires acceptance: Change is about being. It begins with accepting yourself just the way you are.

Table 1.2

Change	Trying Harder	Not Trying So Hard
Anger management	Setting up rewards for controlling your anger and punishments for acting inappropriately; taking "timeouts"	Working to understand the inner conflicts that lead to frustration; looking at your need to be in control
Weight management	Controlled eating; planned or prepared meals	Intuitive eating: paying close attention to your level of hunger and eating when you are hungry and what you want to eat
Over-spending	Budgeting, cutting up credit cards, going to cash only system for discretionary spending	Looking for ways to satisfying the inner emptiness and loneliness that may be driving the spending
Needing to earn more money	Assertiveness classes, meeting with a recruiter, hiring a job coach	Trying to identify your internal obstacles to success; becoming more comfortable with being successful and treating yourself well
Wanting to feel closer to your life partner	Practicing communication skills, planning a regular "date night"	Looking at your own resistance and fears about intimacy

You might turn to the professional literature hoping for a more objective perspective, but unfortunately, you will run into the same bias. Proponents of various schools of psychotherapy regularly make claims for the superiority of their approach, but research done by scientists with no theoretical allegiance indicates all approaches are about equally effective.[10] Arguments about the superiority of various approaches to change are of interest primarily to academics and self-help gurus. What you want to know is "What is the best way for me to make this particular change at this time in my life?"

An old Sufi story tells about two people who brought their case before a judge. The first man presented his side and the judge said, "Yes, you are right." The second man pled his case and again the judge responded, "Yes, you are right." Exasperated, the clerk of the court stood and said, "Wait a minute, they can't both be right." The judge calmly replied, "Yes, you are right."

Some people like the thrill of upwind sailing, while others prefer the calm stability of sailing downwind. Both are perfectly fine ways to sail, and it does not matter much until you commit to a particular direction. At the end of my day of sailing, I had to find a spot to anchor for the night. If I wanted to anchor somewhere further north, then the exhilarating hard work of sailing upwind was the best way to get there. If I chose to anchor further south then a relaxed downwind sail was the best way to go. Whatever direction I chose would determine the type of sailing I needed to do. Some course changes are best accomplished by Trying Harder and others by Not Trying So Hard.

Let us look at the stories of two people, Tom and Barbara, in order to better understand how these two approaches actually work in people's lives.

LOOKING FOR LOVE IN ALL THE WRONG PLACES

Trying Harder

If at first you don't succeed, try, try again.

—Thomas Palmer, American educator (1840)[11]

Tom is twenty-nine years old, recently divorced, and very lonely. He was married for seven years and has a five-year-old son and a two-and-a-half-year-old daughter. Tom was very shy in high school and did not date much. Tom met his wife when he was a senior in high school; they dated through college and married as soon as they graduated.

This is the first time Tom has ever really been alone in his life. Tom feels a rising sense of anxiety verging on panic whenever he does not have his children with him or cannot find some activity to distract himself. Growing up, Tom's family talked a lot about loving each other, but they did not always act in ways that matched what they said. Neither of Tom's parents abused or mistreated him, but when Tom turned to his parents for emotional support, they often seemed preoccupied with their own concerns, and frequently did not have time for him. Tom's mother thinks it's amusing to tell stories about how he clung to her for dear life on the first day of kindergarten, and what a difficult time they had leaving Tom with a babysitter.

As a newly single adult, Tom is re-experiencing some of those same feelings of distress about being alone that he felt in childhood. Normally a social drinker, Tom began to have a glass of wine with dinner every night, and was distressed to notice one glass often became two, and occasionally three. To his credit, Tom decided to take responsibility for changing his life by facing his fears of being alone.

Tom is a smart and capable man. His parents were pull-yourself-up-by-your-bootstraps kinds of people who firmly believed hard work was the solution to any life problem. If happiness equals the distance between the way things are and the way you expect them to be, Tom's parents believed the path to happiness lay in changing the way things are.

Tom reasoned he had picked poorly in his first marriage because he had simply followed his heart and had not dated enough to make a more careful choice. This time, Tom decided to use his good analytic skills to help him find a partner. He figured finding a wife was a lot like sales work. Tom knew from experience for every twenty sales calls he made, about one customer would agree to meet with him, and for every ten customers who met with him he would close one sale. Tom thought the more dates he went on, the better his chances of meeting the right woman.

Tom went to his local bookstore and bought a number of books about dating, and how to find the person who is right for you. He joined a local running club and a gourmet-dining group, hoping to meet a woman who shared his interests. Tom met a few women and went out on several dates. Awkward and uncomfortable at first, Tom eventually began to feel more relaxed and even began to enjoy himself a bit. After several months, Tom still had not met anyone he was interested in seeing more than a few times. He decided the problem was he still was not meeting enough women, so Tom decided to Try Harder.

Tom carefully researched, and then joined an Internet dating site. He painstakingly filled out the lengthy personality questionnaire promising to match him with compatible women. Tom met a lot more women and went out on three to four dates a week. He dated some women several times, but most did not warrant a second look. No one really stood out.

Tom used the Trying Harder approach to change, which is based on the premise that while change is natural it is not always easy, so we often have to do something intentionally to change our lives. We are a culture of doing, not being. We say "don't just sit there, do something." When Tom felt anxious about being alone, he assumed it would take more effort to get out and meet people.

The Advantages of Trying Harder

It is common sense to take a method and try it. If it fails, admit it frankly and try another. But above all, try something.

—Franklin D. Roosevelt[12]

Trying Harder is about change from the outside in, changing how you behave, or changing the external circumstances of your life in order to change yourself. Trying Harder is a powerful approach to problem solving that can lead to rapid and significant change. Millions of people have made substantial and enduring changes in their lives by refusing to give up and persisting through incredible obstacles and adversity. People have lost hundreds of pounds and kept the weight off, recovered from diseases said to be terminal, and found love in their lives after years of pain and loneliness.

Trying Harder is effective because it helps us to embrace our experience from the outside in. For example, if a dog bit you as a child you may develop a phobia and avoid all contact with dogs. In order to get over your fear you need to experience being with dogs in a way that is safe, but your phobia prevents you from having the very experience needed to change. Many effective phobia treatments work from the outside in, gradually reintroducing you to the situation you have been avoiding so you can re-experience that situation as safe.

Trying Harder is the approach that is most familiar to us in the West. America is the Land of Opportunity. We are a country founded by Europeans escaping an aristocracy in which one's station in life was limited by birth, in order to found a meritocracy in which hard work could overcome any obstacle, where anyone can be president or become a millionaire. Americans see hard work as the great equalizer; we admire industry over ability. President Clinton understood this, so instead of reminding us he was the only president who was a Rhodes Scholar, he emphasized how he overcame his humble beginnings through hard work.

Trying Harder is the natural choice for Tom because it is what he is most familiar with; it is what his parents taught him by example to do when there is something you want to change about your life. Most of us are just like Tom; regardless of what advice we receive or what we rationally believe would be the best approach, we are all likely to start with the approach to change most comfortable and familiar to us.

Trying Harder appeals to us because working at change from the outside in often produces immediate and tangible evidence we are changing and gives us a sense of control and mastery in our lives. It just feels good to see something is changing. We are also more likely to get support and reinforcement from others, because our efforts to change and the results are more visible than if we approach change from the inside out. The people around us are also likely to be more invested in our changing from the outside in, because it is our behavior, more than the way we feel, that has the most direct impact on them.

The Limitations of Trying Harder

The best laid schemes o' mice and men
  Gang aft a-gley
  An' lea'e us nought but grief an' pain,
  For promised joy

—Robert Burns[13]

While Trying Harder is often a powerfully effective way to change your life, times also arise when you are just not going to get where you are headed no matter how hard you try. For example, some couples spend years exhausting every outside in means available to conceive a child, and then are pleasantly surprised to learn they are pregnant soon after giving up on the idea of having a biological child. The biology is the same; the only thing that changed was the couples' internal shift in deciding to Stop Trying So Hard. Having something "on the tip of your tongue" is an everyday example; the harder you try to remember what you were thinking of, the less likely you are to remember, but as soon as you Stop Trying So Hard it usually pops right into your head.

If you have ever had trouble falling asleep, you know very well that Trying Harder only makes it more difficult. I worked with a woman named Susan who had a hard time falling asleep because as soon as she lay down she felt terribly anxious and her thoughts raced. She tried to force the anxiety from her mind or distract herself by thinking about something else, but nothing worked. I told her that her anxiety suggested something was pressing into her awareness and trying to get her attention. Rather than Trying Harder to banish the experience, I suggested she pay attention to her experience and see what she could learn. Susan returned the next week and told me my suggestion was initially very frustrating. She lay in bed for hours the first night with no new understanding of what was keeping her awake. Just as she was drifting off to sleep, however, the thought came to Susan that she was worried about her fourteen-year-old daughter. Although Susan could not think of any reason for her concern, Susan talked to her daughter the next day, only to discover her daughter had been struggling with her closest group of friends and it was starting to influence how she felt about herself.

It is difficult for us to imagine Trying Harder will not succeed eventually, as Vince Lombardi said, "Winners never quit, and quitters never win." Despite his iconic status, Lombardi actually got it wrong. Research suggests people who quit in the face of unobtainable goals suffered fewer health problems and showed fewer signs of psychological stress than those who resisted quitting.[14]

When we get stuck we tend to keep doing more of the same, even when that is clearly not working and there is no indication it ever will, repeatedly forgetting that one definition of *insanity* is doing the same thing over and over again expecting different results. The "sunk cost fallacy" refers to the universal human tendency to justify our mistakes by throwing good money after bad.[15] When Toad's seeds did not come up right away, he assumed he needed to Try Harder; when lighting the candles for his seeds did not work; he sat up with them all night and read his seeds stories and sang songs to them. It did not occur to Toad that none of his determined efforts would ever help his seeds to grow, no matter how hard he tried.

Persisting in Trying Harder can not only be ineffective; it can actually make things worse by creating a backlash, which occurs when you blame yourself for failing to change something that seems simple and straightforward on the outside, but is actually very complex internally. Researchers confirm that moving prematurely to a Trying Harder approach often makes the situation worse.[16] For example, believing losing weight is simple because all you have to do is eat less and exercise is a dangerous oversimplification that can lead to weight gain rather than loss. Similarly, believing that getting on top of your finances should be straightforward because all you have to do is set aside the time and get it done can increase rather than decrease your debt. Any self-help program that endorses only Trying Harder strategies can do more harm than good. If you start with the assumption that Trying Harder can overcome any problem, the unfortunate corollary is it must be your fault if you are not changing, because you should be able to change if you only try hard enough.

As the months went by without meeting anyone special, Tom began to blame himself for not doing whatever it took to meet the right person. Tom started to wonder what might be wrong with him if he was not attracting the kind of women he wanted to meet. Tom did not much like the women he was dating, and worse, he began to not like himself much either. Every date started to seem like a dull and perfunctory exchange of life stories, feigning interest while interviewing each other as if they were applicants for the position of life partner. Dating was more like a chore than an adventure, more like a business transaction than a courtship. The more Tom dated, the more he despaired of ever meeting someone special. He wondered how anything intimate, much less magical, could come from such stilted exchanges.

Not Trying So Hard

> If at first you don't succeed, try again. Then quit. No use being a
> damn fool about it.
>
> —W.C. Fields[17]

> The first rule of holes: When you are in one, quit digging.
>
> —Molly Ivins[18]

Tom's good friend Barbara is also single, but she is going about dating
in an entirely different way. Barbara kept telling Tom he would never
meet someone until he Stops Trying So Hard. Barbara suggested that
Tom just relax and be himself, rather than Trying So Hard to be the
person he thinks will be attractive to other people.

Not Trying So Hard is about change from the inside out, embracing
our internal experience in order to change how we act in the world. In
the touching film, *My Big Fat Greek Wedding,* a daughter laments that
her mother does not challenge her husband's contention he is the "head
of the family." The mother replies that while her husband is the head
of the family, she, the mother, is the neck of the family, and points out
that whichever way the neck points the head has to follow. The way we
behave is the "head" of the family that inevitably follows the "neck" of
our internal experience.

Our reluctance to embrace Not Trying So Hard reflects an underlying puritanical distrust of ourselves. On some levels, we believe if we do
not push ourselves, that we will not do what we need to do to change. To
change by Not Trying So Hard we have to let go of our plans and agendas and follow our deeper internal wisdom, allowing the natural process
of change to unfold in often unanticipated and mysterious ways. When
a baseball pitcher is in a groove and throwing strikes, he may say it felt
"effortless," he just "reared back and threw strikes." When his control is
off the coach may tell him he is "aiming the ball" or "trying to over-think
it." A good pitcher understands accuracy starts within, and Trying Too
Hard can make it more difficult to throw strikes.

Thoreau wrote, "Not until we are lost do we begin to understand
ourselves." One night I was out walking with my wife and she lost an
earring that was precious to her. I got a flashlight and we spent an hour

looking for the earring. We did everything we knew to do. Finally, I remembered having heard a quote from Carl Jung earlier that same day about not being able to find something until you quit looking for it. I shared this idea with my wife. We turned off the flashlight, stopped looking for the earring, and started back for home. As I turned around, I felt the earring under my bare foot with the very first step I took. I am quite sure the earring had been there all along, but I could not see it as long as I was Trying So Hard to find it.

Not Trying So Hard is about inviting change into our lives, because as with any lover, when we pursue change too ardently we risk pushing her farther away. Sometimes change is what happens while we are waiting to change. Tom saw the wisdom in what Barbara was saying about not Trying So Hard, but Tom was raised to think of Not Trying So Hard as just being lazy. His dad would often say, "Quitters don't win, and winners don't quit." Tom knew most of what he had accomplished in his life came from hard work, and giving up did not seem like it would solve anything.

Because we equate change with action in this culture, Not Trying So Hard can seem like passivity. The crowd always cheers for the home team to go for it on fourth down, regardless of the risk. President Carter's popularity ratings plummeted while he negotiated the hostage crisis in Iran rather than taking military action, whereas President Ronald Reagan's popularity soared when he took preemptive action to rescue the hostages.[19]

Not Trying So Hard is not just passively waiting for something to happen, but rather, as theologian Henri Nouwen described, "a patience that asks us to live the moment to the fullest to be completely present to the moment, to taste the here and now, to be where we are."[20] Nouwen continues, "When we are impatient, we try to get away from where we are. We behave as if the real thing will happen tomorrow, later, and somewhere else." He exhorts us to "be patient and trust that the treasure we look for is hidden in the ground on which we stand."

Not Trying So Hard seems counterintuitive to us. We are skeptical about change from the inside out. We are skeptical that shifts in internal experience alone can lead to concrete, observable change in our lives. We have more faith in things we can see, touch, or count. Oncologist and author Rachel Naomi Remen told a group of physicians about a woman diagnosed with terminal cancer and given three months to live. The woman discontinued all medical treatments and pursued a rigorous course of prayer, meditation, and other forms of spiritual healing. She returned to the physician's office three months later cancer free. Remen asked the group how they accounted for this, and they all agreed that the original diagnosis had been incorrect. It simply did not occur to them that her inside-out approach could have healed her cancer.

Despite overwhelming scientific evidence, we remain skeptical about the effectiveness of inside-out approaches to change. We tend to write it off to the patient just subjectively believing he or she is better, but not really being objectively being better. For example, most placebo research looks at subjective phenomenon such as pain that cannot be measured objectively. However, research suggests that active placebos are effective as much as seventy percent of the time, and not just with subjective symptoms such as pain but also with objective physiological changes such as dilation of airways in asthmatics or colon inflammation in patients with colitis. In fact, several significant medical procedures were discontinued because they were no more effective than a placebo.[21]

Conversely, hopelessness, which is the absence of the belief active in placebos, can dramatically interfere with or even block the process of change. For example, hopelessness is a risk factor for developing cancer and is related to greater tumor progression and earlier death in cancer patients.[22] In one study, moderately hopeless men had more then three times the risk of death, primarily from cardiovascular disease and cancer, than did men who were more hopeful.[23]

How do we account for these shifts in internal experience leading to objective external change? It may be that our internal belief that we can change activates our innate self-healing mechanisms, which research suggests are the primary factor responsible for all change.[24] An orthopedic surgeon became interested in placebos. He took ten patients scheduled for arthroscopic surgery to relieve arthritis pain in their knees, and divided them into three groups. One group underwent the standard arthroscopic surgery—scraping and rinsing of the knee joint; the second group had the rinsing procedure alone; and in the third group the physician made three incisions in the patient's knee to create the impression they had surgery, but no surgery was performed. Six months after the experiment, all of the patients reported much less pain and none were dissatisfied with the outcome.[25]

On one level, we can think of this as evidence for the power of belief to shift our internal, subjective experience. From this perspective, the outside-in surgical procedure was responsible for the change and the inside-out placebo effect mimicked or enhanced these outside-in treatment effects. This understanding rests on the assumption that the patients who had the surgery felt less pain because they had had the surgical procedure and the patients who did not have surgery felt better because they believed they would. Consider the possibility, however, that all three groups of patients felt better because their belief in the efficacy of the procedure activated their own internal healing mechanisms, and that the patients who had the surgical procedure got better because they expected to.

One of my favorite experiences as a therapist is to learn that my inside-out work with a patient has resulted in significant life changes without our ever talking about it. For example, I worked with a woman who was severely traumatized and able to leave her home only for her weekly psychotherapy appointments and occasional errands. Our work together focused almost exclusively on her in-the-moment experience during the session, and we rarely talked about her daily life outside of therapy. One day, after several years of therapy, she mentioned in passing conflict with someone at her health club. Puzzled, I asked when she had joined a health club, and she told me she started going to the gym daily six months ago and was attending church weekly.

Despite his best intentions to keep Trying Harder to change, Tom found himself continually making excuses to avoid dating. It seemed like a lot of trouble whenever a new woman contacted Tom by e-mail, and going out with friends or even staying home with a good book seemed a lot more appealing. Tom eventually quit all the activities he had been doing to meet single women, and even removed his personal ad from the Internet.

Tom developed a close group of friends and spent a lot of his free time with them. In his frenetic rush to fill the loneliness in his life Tom had rarely taken time to allow himself to feel, much less share with anyone how sad he was about being alone, and how scared he was that he would never find a partner. Tom got more comfortable over time opening up with his new friends, and somehow they understood and accepted how he felt. Tom noticed the more time he spent with people who cared about him the more he started to care about himself, and the more Tom cared about himself the less time he spent thinking about meeting women and getting married.

Tom continued to date from time to time, but his dates felt more relaxed, more like meeting a new friend. Tom went out with some women several times, but forged no special connection with any of them. Tom even became good friends with a woman he dated a few times, something that would have been unimaginable before. Dating was not so emotionally charged for Tom because the stakes were not as high; Tom did not feel so desperate or emotionally preoccupied with meeting someone.

Tom was more content with his life than he ever remembered being, happier than he had ever been when he was married, and much happier than he thought it was possible to be without a woman with whom to share his life. One Sunday morning, Tom had just gone for a run and was relaxing and reading the paper at a neighborhood café. A nice looking woman, Mary, walked in and asked Tom if she could share his table with him. Without thinking much about it, Tom agreed. The two of them struck up a conversation. Tom was very relaxed and just being himself because he was not expecting anything to come of this chance encounter. Tom was so comfortable talking with Mary they sat there talking for over three hours before they knew it.

Tom realized something felt different about being with Mary, different from his experiences with all the other women he had dated. Tom felt comfortable being himself with Mary in ways he had never been with anyone else, including his ex-wife. Mary asked Tom if he would like to have dinner together later that night, and Tom quickly agreed because it seemed like the most natural thing in the world to continue being together. Tom and Mary have been seeing each other regularly for the past four months, and the special connection they shared that day has grown stronger for both of them. While they have had their share of arguments and upsets, both Tom and Mary are clear they have found someone special in their lives and they are both hopeful about sharing a future together.

Tom started out Trying Harder. That is a perfectly reasonable approach, one that has worked for many people with the very same problem, but it was not very effective for Tom. Maybe Tom's parents were right that winners never quit. Maybe Tom gave up too soon and he would have been successful if had kept Trying Harder. How could Tom know if hanging in there would work eventually or if he was never going to succeed no matter how hard he tried? Would Tom have met someone sooner if he began by Not Trying So Hard? Let us look at Tom's friend, Barbara, who is also looking for a life partner but going about it in a different way.

Barbara is thirty-one years old, and has never been married. Barbara dates from time to time, and has enjoyed a number of long-term committed relationships. Barbara has a job that is challenging and meaningful, her friendships are rich and intimate, and she is very involved with her neighborhood association, her church, and a variety of social action projects. Barbara genuinely does want to find someone to settle down and raise a family with, but she is determined not to become like some of her friends who in middle school Barbara would have called "boy crazy." It seems to Barbara some of her friends are so focused on the promised land of a husband and a family they are not enjoying much of their lives here on earth. Barbara also gets her feelings hurt regularly when friends cancel plans with her at the last minute to go out with a guy they have just met.

Barbara grew up in a home that was a little countercultural. Her parents, disenchanted with the Protestant faiths of their childhood, got interested in Eastern religions, yoga, and meditation. They taught Barbara to "go with the flow" and "trust the universe." If happiness is the distance between the way things are and the way you expect them to be, Barbara's parents sought happiness by trying to change their expectations of how things should be.

Barbara has always believed she will find the right guy whenever she is internally ready. Barbara is very satisfied with her rich and full life, while her friends who focus more on dating often complain about being lonely and unhappy. On top of that, most of Barbara's friends who are trying so hard to get married are still single. It seems to Barbara like they are giving up a lot and not getting much in return. Most of the long-term couples Barbara knows met each other serendipitously, like Tom and Mary. Barbara believes Trying So Hard is actually a big part of why her friends are not meeting the right person. Barbara's grandmother liked to say, "A watched pot never boils." Barbara is confident if she does not force things, and simply continues to live a life that is authentic and reflects who she truly is, that she will eventually find just what she needs.

One of the challenges of Not Trying So Hard is that it requires a lot of patience because when you are in a lot of emotional distress, the desire to do something is compelling. Deeply ingrained patterns can be difficult to change by Not Trying So Hard alone, and it is difficult to know when to be patient and when action is required. Much of twelve-step recovery programs are about patient inside-out change, but they also recognize the importance of integrating outside-in strategies like "act as if." In other words, behave as if you are internally ready for sobriety until you actually are ready.[26]

There is an old joke about a man who prayed to God every day for something new. On Monday, he prayed for a new car, Tuesday for a bigger house, Wednesday for a promotion, and so on. This went on for years and years, but none of his prayers were answered. One day, exasperated, he beseeched God: "God, all of these years my prayers have gone unanswered. Please, if you will just answer this one prayer, if you will just let me win the lottery I promise to never bother you again." All of a sudden, there was thunder and lightening from the heavens, and God spoke; "Would you meet me half way? Would you at least buy a ticket?" It is fine for Barbara to focus on getting internally ready for a relationship, but at some point, she may need to use the same kind of outside-in strategies Tom used to put her in a position to meet people. She may need to buy a ticket.

After they had been dating for a couple of months, Tom introduced Mary to Barbara and his other friends. Most of Tom's friends thought Mary was wonderful, and they all commented they had never seen Tom so happy. Barbara, on the other hand, was surprised and somewhat distressed that she did not like Mary as much as much as she had hoped to. Barbara could not figure out why she was spending so much time and energy categorizing all of Mary's imagined faults, and listing all of the reasons why Mary wasn't good enough for Tom and why their relationship would never work.

Barbara got an invitation to attend the wedding of another close friend, and once again, Barbara was surprised by her internal reaction.

Barbara became increasingly apprehensive as the date of the wedding approached, and started to come up with all sorts of reasons not to go. At the ceremony Barbara started crying; not the kind of polite crying people often do at weddings, but a deep, chest-wracking can't-catch-your-breath kind of sobbing that seemed like it would never end.

That same night Barbara had a very disturbing dream. In her dream, Barbara was lost in a strange city. She saw herself in the reflection of a storefront window and was shocked to see she was emaciated and looked as if she had been living on the streets for years. In her dream, Barbara realized she was absolutely starving. Everyone walking by her was eating all kinds of delicious looking food: sandwiches, pizza, hamburgers, and hot dogs. Barbara wanted desperately to ask someone to share their food with her, but she was paralyzed, surrounded by food but unable to reach out and ask for any. Some of the people walking by even seemed to be trying to offer their food to Barbara, but she was mute, unable to speak up and let anyone know how hungry she was.

Barbara awoke inspired. Barbara believed her dream meant that while much of her life was very full, she had not been feeding herself well, and her longing for a life partner was much stronger than she had let herself know. Furthermore, Barbara's dream told her she would need help from others to fill this need, and the help she needed was available all around her if she could only get herself to reach out. To do that, Barbara knew she would have to Try Harder; she decided to buy a ticket.

Barbara began to tell everyone she knew she wanted to meet someone special, and she asked people directly to introduce her to eligible men. Barbara joined the singles group at her church she had previously avoided. When Barbara heard the grocery store was the new hot place for singles to meet she found herself making extra trips to pick up the little things she had "forgotten," and then lingering in the frozen dinners section where she figured single men would be most likely to shop. Barbara even threw herself into online dating, something she swore she would never do. Barbara registered with three different dating sites, and while she did meet a lot of guys, none of them were the kind of person Barbara could imagine spending her life with. Barbara then hired a consultant to help her craft a profile that would attract just the kind of person she was most interested in meeting.

Sure enough, there was a noticeable shift in the kind of men Barbara started to meet. Her dates were more and more interesting, and she began to meet people she was interested in getting to know better. After a few months, Barbara was a veteran of the dating wars, but when she met Ralph, Barbara recognized right away that there was something very special between them. Unbelievably, they met in the grocery store—you guessed it, in the frozen dinner aisle.

Barbara was caught off guard by the strength of her feelings for Ralph. She felt like the lovesick schoolgirl she had never really allowed herself to be. Barbara thought of Ralph all the time, sent him silly little emails and text messages, and saw him almost every day. Barbara was particularly surprised at how much she missed Ralph when they spent even a day or two apart. After about a year Barbara and Ralph were both clear they had found the special person they wanted to spend the rest of their lives with.

CONCLUSIONS

Tom and Barbara are friends who used two very different approaches to solve the same problem. Tom started out Trying Harder. When that did not work, Tom tried to hold onto his old way of doing things, but gradually and often without realizing it Tom Stopped Trying So Hard, which eventually lead to his meeting Mary. Barbara, on the other hand, started out Not Trying So Hard. Barbara thought that was working pretty well for her until she realized the strength of her internal dissatisfaction and made a conscious decision to start Trying Harder, which resulted in her meeting Ralph.

Countless people have made important life changes by Trying Harder, by persisting in the face of enormous obstacles until they finally succeeded, like the people who try to quit smoking for years using every device and program imaginable until they finally succeed. Of course, many other people who are equally sincere in their efforts to quit smoking using the exact same methods have never succeeded. Innumerable people have also made significant changes in their lives by Not Trying So Hard, like the people with heart problems who have tried unsuccessfully for years to change their diets and start a regular exercise program, only to succeed overnight when their physician told them they would need coronary bypass surgery if they did not change their lifestyle.

Why is Trying Harder effective for some people and not for others? Would everyone eventually be able to change if they persisted in Trying Harder, or do we sometimes get stuck in a revolving door and will never change no matter how hard we try? Would Not Trying So Hard work for everyone if he or she stuck with it, or are there times when you just have to dig in and push yourself to change?

There is an old saying: "If you give a man a fish you have fed him for today, but if you teach a man to fish you have fed him for a lifetime." When we advocate for one particular approach to change, then we are only feeding people for today. Extensive psychological research makes it clear that neither Trying Harder nor Not Trying So Hard by itself is as effective as learning how to use the two approaches together.[27] The aim of this book is to teach you how to fish so that you have the skills to make the changes you want to see in your life over time, and across a wide variety of situations. The purpose of this book is to teach you how to make effective and enduring change in your life by learning when to Try Harder and when to Stop Trying So Hard.

2

EMBRACE EXPERIENCE

Listen to the voice of experience,
   It has the most truth.

—Chinese fortune cookie

There has been a long-standing turf war in psychology and other fields between advocates of the Trying Harder and Not Trying So Hard approaches to change. Contrary to the self-promoting claims of both approaches, research consistently shows that neither Trying Harder nor Not Trying So Hard is a more effective approach to change.[1] Most of us just want to know the best way to create and sustain the kind of change we want to see in our lives.

There is an old saying, "When all you have is a hammer, everything looks like a nail." Advocating for one particular approach to change is like giving you a hammer and telling you to use this one tool for all the different kinds of change you want to make in your life. This strategy is bound to be effective occasionally; after all, a hammer is a very effective life tool if you happen to be driving nails. On the other hand, if you are not driving nails, if you are trying to screw two boards together, then being limited to a hammer is frustrating. You might even start to blame yourself if you do not understand that the problem is not having the right tool for the right job. Ideally, you will have a variety of tools in your toolbox, as well an understanding of how to use each tool and which tool is most effective for different jobs. Learning how to make effective and enduring change over time and across a wide range of life situations requires not the mastery of any particular approach to change but an understanding of the process that underlies all change, and understanding when to Try Harder and when to Stop Trying So Hard.

The trend in psychological research is a movement away from the competitive analysis of various therapeutic techniques and a growing emphasis on understanding the factors accounting for change across people and settings. The central premise of this book is that the common factor underlying all approaches to change is the process of embracing experience.

Embracing experience means being present in our lives, engaging and moving further into our experience of the moment: our thoughts, feelings, fantasies, memories, physical sensations, intuitions, and so on. All approaches to change are different ways to help people embrace their experience more fully. Psychotherapy is a weekly invitation to embrace your experience. Meditation is a disciplined way to embrace experience. Prayer is another way to embrace experience, particularly if you think of prayer as listening as well as speaking.

Embracing experience requires more than just showing up. It is quite possible to go through powerful life situations without allowing them to affect you, without allowing the experiences to penetrate. Embracing experience involves fully immersing yourself in your experience of the moment, indwelling your experience, giving yourself over to your experience as you live it. I traveled Europe as a young man, and one of my most emotionally powerful experiences was seeing the Sistine Chapel. Afterward, I sat in the plaza outside, reverberating with what for me was a profoundly spiritual experience. I overheard two other travelers commenting that the quality of the slides they had bought was so professional that it might have been just as good to stay home and buy the slides. Although we had physically been inside the same chapel, we clearly had very different experiences.

Embracing experience refers to our *prereflective experience*,[2] that is, our experience as we live it prior to our thoughts and reflections about our experience because we have to step outside of our lived experience in order to reflect on it. In the biblical story of creation, Adam and Eve were in the paradise of pure lived experience until they stepped out of their experience by eating of the tree of knowledge. When they reflected on their lives for the first time, they knew the experience of shame, the experience of seeing themselves from the outside. There is a well-known beer commercial in which a group of men is quietly sharing a bonding experience around a campfire. One of them says, "It just doesn't get any better than this," but the experience was better right before one of them stepped outside of the experience to reflect on it.

Embracing experience also requires setting aside what others expect us to experience, and what we ourselves expect to experience in order to embrace authentically our experience as we actually live it. Let's look at the example of Ken. Whenever Ken visited his family, he was uncharacteristically quiet and deferential. Although he is an exceptionally bright and competent man, Ken's family is very critical of him, and when he is with them Ken regresses and becomes the person his family expects him to be. Ken's most recent visit home came shortly after he got a big promotion at work. Ken told his parents about the promotion with a great deal of excitement and pride. As his parents subtly picked away at Ken's accomplishment, Ken literally felt the energy draining from his body. Ken paused in the middle of the conversation, closed his eyes for a moment, and remembered when the president of the company announced his promotion to the whole company. Embracing the memory of that experience helped Ken to return to the conversation with his parents, feeling less anxious and more like himself.

Embracing experience is sometimes easier to recognize in its absence than in its presence, as in the person who only becomes aware of how much he cares for a loved one after the loved one has died, or the man who gets angry because he has difficulty embracing the experience of feeling hurt. Other examples are the woman who has difficulty setting limits on her giving to others because she has difficulty embracing her experience of uncertainty, the woman who is quiet and depressed because she has difficulty embracing her experience of being angry with others, or the man who engages in a series of brief relationships because he has difficulty embracing his experience of feeling intimate with others.

The opposite of embracing experience is acting out, that is, any action taken to avoid experience. Drug and alcohol abuse are classic forms of acting out rather than embracing the experience of emotional distress or spiritual emptiness. Extramarital affairs are a way of acting out rather than embracing the experience of interpersonal tension or difficulties with intimacy. Over-functioning and codependency are ways of acting out rather than embracing fears of inadequacy or abandonment. Most of our life struggles are the result of acting out rather than embracing our experience. The therapeutic contract is that both patient and therapist endeavor to put all of our experience into words rather than actions, and to hang in there together toward a positive outcome (D. Dingman, personal communication, 2002).

EXERCISE

Please find a quiet place where you can sit uninterrupted for fifteen to thirty minutes. Do not forget to turn off all the things that might disturb you by ringing or vibrating. Read these instructions through first, and then try the exercise.

Sit quietly in a chair and close your eyes. Take a few deep breaths, expanding your belly to make room for the air coming in, and then exhaling fully, pushing all of the air from your body. Begin to simply pay attention to your experience of the moment: your thoughts, emotions, memories, bodily sensations, images, and so on. Notice any place of tension or discomfort, something that feels unfinished or seems to be calling for your attention. If you are not accustomed to this type of exercise, do not start with something that is very distressing to you right now. It is best to start with something that has some tension but is less threatening and more manageable. Let yourself notice this tension or distress. As you are distracted by thoughts or other sensations, gently bring your attention back to the experience you are trying to embrace. Do not try to change anything about your experience, do not try to figure anything out, or direct your attention in any way. Just continue to pay attention to your ongoing experience.

You will probably notice that some aspects of this experience are more difficult to focus on, thoughts that are troubling, physical sensations or emotions that are uncomfortable, memories that are disturbing, places it is difficult to keep your attention focused. Try to make room for all aspects of this experience; keep bringing your attention gently back to the experience you are trying to embrace. Try not to judge yourself in this process; just notice the aspects of your experience that are more difficult to embrace and keep gently returning your focus back to the full range of the experience you are trying to more fully embrace. Do this gently, like you would in stretching a muscle. Visually imagine yourself making more and more room inside of yourself for all of this experience.

As you go through this process, notice any shifts in your experience. Do you notice a change? If you hang in there and gently keep embracing this part of your experience, you will probably notice something change. If you do not notice a shift in your experience, try the exercise again with something less distressing. If that does not help, you will learn more in chapter 4 about strategies to help you when you get stuck.

CHANGE HAPPENS THROUGH EXPERIENCE

> If a hundred physicians say a man is well, but he says he is sick,
> Then he is sick.
>
> —Old Jewish Saying

Change happens through experience because we all live in the world in a way that matches how we experience the world. We all experience the world in a particular way that is an amalgamation of our histories. The developmental theorist Daniel Stern suggests that by seven months infants have accrued sufficient experience to generalize "an individualized, personal expectation of how things are likely to proceed on a moment-to-moment basis."[3]

Our experience is our reality. Everyone acts in a way that makes sense to him or her, given how that individual sees the world. We do not live our lives based on any ostensibly objective reality; we live in response to our own subjective experience. If you grew up in an environment that was unpredictable and dangerous, whether that was on the streets of Newark or in a violent family, then the world is a dangerous place for you and you will live your life accordingly. If you and I get into an animated political discussion and I start to raise my voice and gesture animatedly, you may get uneasy even if I have never given any indication of being violent or ever done anything to hurt you. It makes sense for you to be more vigilant in situations like this; it would be foolhardy to let down your guard. As a colleague of mine is fond of saying, "Reality is not the issue" (D. Dingman, personal communication, 1998).

If I can understand the way someone sees the world, then I can make sense of how he or she acts. If I do not understand the way someone acts, it is not because the way that person acts does not make sense; it is because I have failed to understand the way that person sees the world. If I saw the world in the same way as that person, I might act in a similar manner.

Here are a set of rules for life written by a young boy from an abusive, alcoholic family:

- Do not trust everybody. People who you can trust will hang around and prove they can be trusted. People who cannot be trusted will not stay around to prove trust. They will say stuff like, "Don't you trust me?" so you have to say no. And they will go but good people will stay to show you.
- Test people and listen good. If you listen good you will hear lies. When you hear lies get away. Test people with stuff that is not important.
- Watch people but don't look at them. Then they think you cannot see them but you can. Then they will do stuff but you really see. And when you see bad, get away.
- Do not tell people everything at one time. Tell them a little bit but not everything. If they do not believe you, get away. If they laugh at you get away. If they use it against you get away.
- Do not love people fast. Fast love is not good love. Fast love is not honest. People who love you and do not know you will love you because they want to hurt you.
- If you do not feel the good way run fast. That means they are bad. If you feel icky inside run very fast (A. Gustin, personal communication, 1991).

Information alone is unlikely to change the way we see the world.[4] Charles Darwin said after witnessing a devastating earthquake, "In one second of time [it] has created in the mind a strong insecurity, which hours of reflection would not have produced."[5] On the side of every pack of cigarettes is a warning from the surgeon general that in essence says, "Smoke these and you will die." That dramatic warning is not enough to get most smokers to quit because they have become impervious to the information; it does not penetrate to the level of their experience.

In the end, our behavior always lines up with our experience. Everyone acts in a way that makes sense to them, given how they see the world. You might be able to force yourself to act for a while as if you do not think the world is dangerous, but eventually you will revert to a way of behaving that matches your lived experience. It would be crazy not to. Twelve-step recovery programs use the concept of a dry drunk to describe people who have stopped the behavior of drinking but will likely relapse because they are not sober; they still experience the world as an alcoholic.[6]

It is only when we begin to experience the world differently that we can start to live in the world differently. In *The Miracle Worker*, the story of Helen Keller, a young girl born both deaf and blind,[7] Helen's family expected very little of her, and Helen defiantly lived down to those expectations. The family hired a tutor to teach Helen sign language, but while Helen was able to parrot the signs for a number of words, she seemed to have no real interest in learning. She just did not get it. One day her tutor ran out of patience, grabbed Helen and pulled her to the well. The tutor splashed water on Helen's face while repeating the sign for water repeatedly. The miracle is that Helen got it; she equated the experience of the water on her face with the sign that represents it. Change happens through experience.

Let's look at the example of Mary. Mary's father was a troubled man who tried to escape his unhappiness by drinking and losing himself in his work. Mary's mother felt lonely and abandoned in her marriage, and responded by withdrawing into depression. As a result, there was very little emotional attention left over for Mary as a child. Her parents did not spend much time with Mary; they were not particularly warm or nurturing with her; and, perhaps most troubling, Mary's parents never seemed to get any pleasure from being with her. Mary concluded that her parents did not like her very much, which was a reasonable conclusion given her early experiences. Beyond that, Mary decided that if her parents did not like her that it must be because she was not a very likable person. How could she come to any other conclusion? After all, the most significant people in Mary's life did not seem to like her, so it was easy for her to believe that she was not very likable.

I still recall the first time I spent the night at a friend's house, and how shocked I was to discover the ways in which his family was fundamentally different from mine, ways in which it had not even occurred to me families could differ. The formula to make someone crazy is to systematically undermine her experience of the world, then seal all of the exits, and not allow her to check her experience with anyone else. As long as Mary had nowhere to go to check the reality of her experience, it would be very difficult for her to come to any other conclusion. In navigation, you need two fixed points to know where you are. With only one source of information, you are hopelessly lost.

Throughout her life, Mary met people who liked her and people who did not, had experiences that confirmed her belief she is unlikable and experiences that challenged that belief. You might think that believing she is likable would be more rewarding, so Mary would pay more attention to the times someone did like her and try to ignore those times when someone did not like her. Unfortunately, Mary started every encounter with the belief that she was unlikable, and that view of herself colored all of her interpersonal experiences. As a result, Mary actually paid more attention to the times when someone did not like her, and often misinterpreted or completely missed instances when someone did like her. Mary managed to convince herself that they really did not like her, or that they were just pretending to like her, or that one person who seemed to like her was merely an exception to her overriding belief, which remained unchallenged. Even worse, Mary's anticipation that other people would not like her often led her to be preemptively hostile and withdrawn, creating a self-fulfilling prophecy. Mary was stuck because her assumptions about being unlikable were interfering with her ability to experience people liking her.

Mary wanted to change how she felt about herself, so she formulated a plan. She made a list of steps she needed to take, and checked off each one in turn. She bought a book on "Learning to Believe You Are Likable" and practiced saying to herself in front of the mirror "I am likable, I am likable" repeatedly. Despite all of Mary's sincere and substantial effort, nothing seemed to work. Mary could not get herself to believe that people really liked her. Nothing seemed to stick. Mary went on believing that she was unlikable, a problem that was compounded now by blaming herself for not being able to change.

Finally, a friend suggested that Mary talk to a therapist. Mary's therapist listened patiently as she recounted her myriad examples of being hurt and disappointed in relationships, and her long list of reasons she was not likable. Rather than disagreeing with Mary or trying to convince her that she was wrong, Mary's therapist asked her to tell him more about her hurt and disappointment.

Over time, an odd thing started to happen. After a while, Mary noticed that she was starting to believe that her therapist liked her. Mary immediately discounted that notion, because after all, her therapist was paid to like her. Nonetheless, the idea that Mary's therapist liked her seemed to grow and take root inside of her. More importantly, when Mary was with her therapist she began to *experience* herself as a likable person.

Over a period of several months, Mary noticed that she was less likely to assume that other people would not like her. She was more able to approach new relationships with fewer expectations, and to see what developed. People found it easier to like Mary, and Mary found it easier to recognize when people did like her and to tolerate the anxiety that was stirred up when people liked her. Over time, Mary got more comfortable with people liking her, and began to build a network of close friends.

Couples most often come to my office complaining that their partner does not do things the right way, but what they really mean is that their partner does not see the world the way that they do. For example, in families in which the mom stays at home to take care of young children, the husband sometimes complains that the house is a mess when he gets home and he can't understand why his wife could not at least straighten up a bit. He is right: he does not understand. He doesn't understand because he has failed to see the world the way his wife sees it, an empathic failure. I often suggest that the wife take a long weekend out of town by herself and leave her husband alone with the kids to take care of all of the tasks that she usually manages during the week, not just to give her a break, but to give him an outside-in empathic experience of seeing the world the way she sees it. Husbands are rarely willing to take me up on this, but when they do they usually get a crash course in seeing the world from their wife's point of view, and after that, things never look the same again.

Noted family therapist Carl Whitaker said that the hardest thing to do in an argument, when you are absolutely one hundred percent convinced that there is not one shred of truth in what your partner is hammering you about, is to find the truth in what she is saying. When couples get to this stuck place with each other, when their allegiance to the way that they see the world is getting in the way of being able to hear the truth in what their partner is saying, I tell them there are three possibilities. Either your partner is psychotic and does not know the difference between reality and fantasy, she is malevolent and making things up just to hurt you, or there is some semblance of truth in what she is trying to tell you and your job is to find out and understand more about that part of the truth.

Does this mean that everything I experience is "real," even if my experience is out of sync with the experiences of others? Don't I need help with my "reality testing?" It is a slippery slope when we start empowering some groups to be the arbitrators of reality, or define reality in consensual terms. Would we support efforts to have African-Americans living in the South during the 1950s define their reality through the eyes of their dominant culture? How about all of the gay people who were miraculously healed when the American Psychiatric Association removed *homosexuality* from the list of psychiatric disorders? Somewhere in between the passivity of accommodation and the egocentrism of assuming one's perception is the sole reality lies the capacity to recognize both the inherent validity of my own experience and the potential divergences between my own experience and that of others.

EXPERIENCE IS DYNAMIC

> Dwell as near as possible to the channel in which your life flows.
>
> —Henry David Thoreau[8]

> One cannot step twice into the same river.
>
> —Heraclitus[9]

Embracing experience facilitates change because our lived experience is like a river, dynamic and flowing, always moving. The word *experi-*

ence comes from the Latin root *per,* meaning "forward" or "through."[10] The river of our experience can move swiftly or meander slowly, sometimes take a straight path, and other times twist in unexpected directions. The water can be smooth and calm or turbulent and rocky, but it is always moving.

Embracing experience is like swimming in the river of life, what Buddhists call "being in the flow."[11] The more we are able to embrace our life experience, to immerse ourselves fully in the flow of our experience, the more we change. The more separated we become from our life experience, the less we change. Change happens through experience.

An old Jewish folk tale captures this wisdom. King Solomon searched his kingdom for a cure for his depression. The king assembled his wise men together. They pondered the problem for a long time and finally gave him a ring engraved with the words "This too shall pass (גם זה יעבור, gam zeh yaavor)." Solomon wore the ring constantly. Every time he felt sad and depressed, he looked at the ring and his mood changed and he felt more cheerful.

Although experience is the royal road to achieving the kind of enduring and effective change we want in our lives, the process of embracing experience can seem counterintuitive at first. Our first instinct is often to pull away from the very experiences we need to change. For example, when we lose a loved one our initial response is often to avoid rather than embrace our emotional pain. However, most of the time it is not our lived experience that is harmful to us. More often, it is all of the machinations we go through to avoid our experience that creates problems in our lives. In thirty years as a practicing psychotherapist, I have yet to meet someone whose experience of grief extended indefinitely. On the other hand, I have worked with a number of people whose inability to allow themselves the experience of grief has restricted the richness of their lives for decades.

As a rule of thumb, I have not tried to protect my children from most naturally occurring life experiences. My son was at his sister's birth when he was three-and-a-half, and my daughter helped shovel the dirt into her grandmother's grave when she was just over one year old. I have been more careful to protect them from what I think of as artificial experiences, like gratuitously violent movies or pornography.

Whenever we disown any aspect of our experience, all we are doing is killing the messenger. The message itself just goes underground, only to emerge later, stronger than ever. An all-too-common example is trying to lose weight by depriving yourself of food, detaching from your experience of hunger, and treating that experience as a weakness to overcome with willpower. You cannot conquer your own experience of hunger indefinitely, and the more you try to suppress that hunger, the more it will return with a vengeance. Three weeks of self-denial lead to an onslaught of binge eating, weight gain, and self-recrimination. Alternatively, extensive research suggests that "intuitive eating" is a very promising new approach to weight management, which encourages people to reject the deprivation model of dieting and attain their "natural weight" by listening to their bodies, by "nurturing your body rather than starving it."[12]

EMBRACING EXPERIENCE BY NOT TRYING SO HARD

All the greatest and most important problems of life are fundamentally insoluble. . . . They can never be solved, but only outgrown.

—Carl G. Jung[13]

We cannot change, we cannot move away from what we are, until we thoroughly accept what we are. Then changes seem to come about almost unnoticed.

—Carl Rogers[14]

Trying Harder and Not Trying So Hard are both effective approaches to change because they are different ways to embrace experience. You can embrace your experience from the inside out by Not Trying So Hard or from the outside in by Trying Harder: two roads that lead to the same place.

Although Not Trying So Hard is the less preferred approach in this culture, it is actually the more direct path to embracing experience. As I discussed in the previous chapter, embracing experience by Not Trying So Hard means letting go of your agendas and your need to have the answer and solve the problem, having the faith to immerse yourself fully in your lived experience of the moment and allow a deeper wisdom to emerge. When you are sad, Not Trying So Hard means embracing your experience of sadness rather than trying to find a way to cheer yourself up, trusting that if you hang in there your experience will shift. When you are angry, embracing your experience by Not Trying So Hard means allowing yourself to experience the depths of your anger rather than trying to talk yourself out of feeling angry because you are worried that other people will not like you.

Let's look at Tim's example. Tim is a bright, hard-working, and capable man who has struggled most of his life with procrastination, both at work and at home. He is profoundly self-critical, even self-loathing at times, judging himself to be a failure for not following through, and being distracted and detached as a father. Over time, Tim and I have tried all kinds of clever Trying Harder strategies, all of which have been unsuccessful and have added to Tim blaming himself for not accomplishing what seemed like such simple solutions.

Eventually I realized I was caught up in Tim's habitually counterproductive Trying Harder approach. I decided it was time to change tacks and try to help Tim Stop Trying So Hard. Tim mentioned a particular task he had been avoiding for some time. I asked Tim to open his calendar and look at the reminder he had been setting for this task, just look at it, breathe, and allow himself to move further into whatever experience he became aware of, without prejudgment or prejudice. Tim quickly went to his most familiar defenses, first fleeing to the past with a series of self-critical judgments about why he had not yet finished this task and then escaping to the future with a series of predictions about never being able to get this or any other task accomplished. Each time I gently redirected Tim back to his experience of the moment, and reminded him to keep breathing and allow himself to enter more fully into his experience of that moment.

Gradually, Tim stopped chattering and grew quieter, and more thoughtful. He began to cry and talk about how terribly, terribly sad he felt to Try So Hard all of his life, and be so frightened that if he did not continue to Try So Hard all of his worst fears about himself would be confirmed. I suggested to Tim that his self-critical judgments and despairing predictions were interfering with embracing his experience of the moment, which seemed to be primarily sadness. I gently invited

Tim to set these derivatives aside (see chapter 5) and allow himself to move further into his experience of sadness.

Tim continued to cry, and said he was thinking about a photograph of his family that his wife gave him. All around the edges of the photograph, his wife wrote all of the wonderful, loving things family members had said about him. I suggested that whenever Tim experienced a self-critical thought he could pause for thirty seconds, remember the picture, and use that image to help him reconnect with his depth of caring and devotion to his family. Tim started carrying the photograph in his briefcase and over the next month reported that it helped significantly with his procrastination both at home and at work.

EMBRACING EXPERIENCE BY TRYING HARDER

> If you want to know the taste of a pear, you must change the pear by eating it yourself. . . . All genuine knowledge originates in direct experience.
>
> —Mao Zedong[15]

While embracing experience by Not Trying So Hard is a powerful way to change, there are times when we have difficulty embracing the experiences we most need to change (see chapter 5). This is when the outside-in approach of Trying Harder can really help us embrace those difficult-to-embrace experiences. For example, Molly was bitten by a dog when she was a small child and is still scared of dogs to this day. To change that fear Molly needs to have a positive, safe experience with a dog, but she is not likely to have that experience because she continues to do everything she can to avoid dogs. We could help Molly get over her fear of dogs from the outside in using systematic desensitization.[16] We might begin by having Molly imagine a dog, and then slowly, step by small step, bring her closer to actually interacting with a dog, each time stopping the procedure and helping her relax whenever she got too anxious. Eventually we could bring Molly to the point where she has a lived experience with a dog that would help change her fear.

Embracing experience by Trying Harder is a bit trickier than Not Trying So Hard because Trying Harder can be used to either embrace or avoid experience. For example, David's wife died six months ago, and he has been having difficulty allowing himself to embrace fully his experience of grief and loss. David's friend, Todd, called, and offered to go with David to visit his wife's grave and help David to get more in touch with his grief, a Trying Harder strategy designed to help David further embrace his experience. On the other hand, David's friend, Fred, called, and said what David needed was to "get back in the saddle" and offered to take David to a singles' mixer, a Trying Harder strategy designed to help David distance from rather than embrace his experience.

Embracing experience by Trying Harder is also more risky than Not Trying So Hard. All of our conscious defenses are organized and prepared for the frontal assault of a Trying Harder approach to change. As a result, embracing experience by Trying Harder can create an unconscious backlash, which can actually make things worse. Chapter 6 goes into more detail about how to avoid creating a backlash when Trying Harder.

Now that you have some understanding of the concept of embracing experience, and how it is used in Trying Harder and Not Trying So Hard approaches, I would like to walk you through four steps of embracing experience: paying attention to your experience, making room for all of your experience, taking responsibility for your experience, and validating your experience. I will also discuss talking about experience, a technique for embracing experience that psychotherapists are particularly fond of, the "talking cure." Finally, you will have an opportunity to practice all that you have learned in this chapter with an exercise that will help you to embrace a specific life experience of your choice.

PAYING ATTENTION TO YOUR EXPERIENCE

> The moment one gives close attention to anything, it becomes a mysterious, awesome, indescribably magnificent world in itself.
>
> —Henry Miller[17]

Embracing experience begins with paying attention to our lives in ways we normally do not. Author Catherine Bateson said that people seek therapy for a wounded capacity to attend.[18] So often, we are physically present but we are not there, we listen but we do not hear, we perceive yet we do not really see. A character in the movie *Postcards from the Edge*[19] wrote a card that said, "Having a wonderful time. Wish I was here."

Every morning I wake up, take my two dogs down to the park, and I read the newspaper for fifteen minutes or so. I notice if it is raining because the paper gets wet, and I notice if it is particularly cold. Otherwise, I do not notice much around me because my attention is focused on the newspaper. One day, the paper was late, so I took the dogs to the park and just walked with them with nothing else to do. I watched the clouds move across the sky, I noticed that the endless humidity of a Southern summer had finally lifted and it was a beautifully cool and crisp autumn day. I also noticed that as I started to pay more attention to the world around me I felt more energized. I realized that I was breathing a little more deeply and that my head felt clearer. The differences were subtle, but I noticed how I changed when I paid closer attention to my experience.

In another example, I generally eat however much food is on my plate at any given meal. I traveled in Europe one summer as a young man. I often ate alone, so I experimented with putting my fork down after every bite. I found I was much clearer about the difference between my experience of physiological hunger, my experience of emotional hunger passing for physiological hunger, and my experience of satiation. As a result, I ate differently. In another daily example, I normally go to bed around the same time every night. If I pause and pay closer attention to my experience before I go to bed, if I pay attention to my experience of being fatigued and needing rest, my experience of lethargy or malaise disguised as fatigue, or my experience of seeking rest to escape some other emotional distress I am avoiding, then I make different decisions about when to go to bed and the quality of my rest is different.

It is not possible to attend fully to every aspect of your lived experience. Our daily efficiency depends on our capacity for selective attention. For example, you literally could not walk if you tried to pay attention to every muscle movement required. Walking requires learning how to attend to some aspects of your experience while ignoring others. Driving is the same way. We have all had the experience of missing an exit on the highway. It is disconcerting initially to realize your attention wandered that much, but good driving requires selective attention.

On the other hand, I went to the gym recently and forgot my work clothes. I put my gym bag in the car, carried my bag into the gym and put it in my locker, worked out, showered, and then only when standing in front of my locker did I first pay attention to the fact that I had no clean clothes to change into. I saw patients all day in sweats and sneakers, and only one person even asked me about it. I am not sure if they were paying as little attention as I was, or if they just did not say anything about it.

Ideally, we are all aiming for a healthy balance between the kind of selective attention that makes daily living more enjoyable and not forgetting your clothes when you go to the gym. Some people are so obsessively focused on the details of their lives that they miss the forest for the trees. They have their budget worked out to the last cent but can't let go enough to enjoy spending any of their money, or they keep track of every conceivable statistic for their child's athletic teams but miss the sheer pleasure of watching their child compete. They need to learn how to pay less attention, to let go of their preoccupation with the details that are interfering with their ability to attend to other, more important aspects of their lives.

Other people have more difficulty getting themselves to pay enough attention. They forget people's names because they were not really paying attention to begin with, or forget their anniversary and put if off to a "bad memory" or being overwhelmed at work when it is really a reflection of taking their loved ones for granted. They need to learn how to set aside some of their habitual distractions enough to be able to pay more attention to the important parts of their lives they are missing.

MAKING ROOM FOR ALL OF YOUR EXPERIENCE

> To heal suffering one must experience it to the full.
>
> —Marcel Proust[20]

Beyond just paying attention to experience, embracing experience also means making room for and accepting all the potential aspects of your experience without judgment or prejudice. We all have areas in which we are more separated from our experience. Like untrained body builders, we develop the areas of our experience we are most familiar and comfortable with, and tend to neglect other aspects of our experience. Men, for example, tend to be more comfortable with the emotional experience of anger, and less familiar with experiencing or sharing vulnerability. As a result, we often express anger when we are feeling vulnerable, which can be very effective in a business negotiation, but is more confusing or even destructive in intimate discourse.

Impasses result from excluding rather than embracing certain aspects of our experience. They are the result of our impaired ability to be more fully all of who we are. Depression is not the result of feeling sad; depression is the result of a restricted capacity to embrace your experience of sadness. Depression is emotional constipation, and the solution is an emotional laxative: the ability to allow all of your experience to move through you naturally.

There are a variety of self-help programs advising people to avoid so-called "negative emotions" such as sadness, fear, or anxiety.[21] In fact, the only valence to our experience is the prejudice we impose. There is no such thing as "positive" or "negative" experiences. There are just the experiences we like and are comfortable with and those we do not like, just as there are not "side effects" of medications, just the effects we like and those we don't (G. H. Williams, personal communication, 2002). The sadness of grieving the loss of a loved one is just as valuable as the sidesplitting hilarity of laughing with a treasured friend. We know the two are more alike than different because we may slide seamlessly from one to the other in intimate conversation. How can sadness and fear be negative emotions when people pay good money to go to the movies hoping to feel sad or scared?

Charlie is a young psychoanalyst who was himself in analysis for a number of years, struggling with the question of his own sexual identity. The idea of accepting himself as a gay man was so intolerable that he became profoundly suicidal. Finally, in despair, he insisted that his analyst consult the founder of the school they had both trained in about why his analysis was not helping him to change his sexual orientation. The consultation that his analyst returned with was, "You are asking the wrong question. You are supposed to have all of your experience." With this simple support for making room for all of his experience, Charlie's years of struggle were over and he was able to accept himself as a gay man.

The same dynamics hold true on a larger systemic level. The most effective solution to any problem emerges from a full hearing of all potential perspectives on the issue, the comfortable and the uncomfortable, the rational and the nonrational, the anticipated and the unanticipated. Research substantiates that heterogeneous groups of people with diverse perspectives can generate effective solutions that no member of the group could generate alone.[22] For example, the Civil Rights and women's movements not only redressed long-standing inequities, but also broadened and enriched our previously truncated national conversation by including the voices of women and minorities.

Psychological symptoms are simply another aspect of our experience to be embraced rather than defeated. Symptoms reflect our deepest unconscious wisdom about what we need to heal. If we try to eliminate the symptom, we risk killing the messenger and losing valuable information. For example, anxiety is often thought of as a symptom, but it is actually just an experience we prefer not to have. We distract ourselves from our anxiety with work, alcohol, or television; but at what cost? We presume that anxiety, like tonsils, should be removed simply because we do not understand its function. When we seek to reduce our anxiety, we are depleting the fuel that spurs us to change the parts of our lives that are no longer working well for us. Similarly, when we attempt to "fix" things for other people, we may deprive them of the anxiety they need to make more substantive and lasting changes in their lives.

TAKING RESPONSIBILITY

God give me the serenity to accept the things I cannot change; Courage to change the things I can; and wisdom to know the difference.

—Reinhold Niebuhr[23]

You must be the change you wish to see in the world.

—Gandhi[24]

How many psychologists does it take to screw in a light bulb? Only one, but first the bulb really has to want to change. Taking responsibility for the change we want to create in our lives means letting go of our lingering infantile fantasies about someone else being responsible for us, like the person who wants something specific for his birthday but doesn't want to tell his partner because "if he really loves me he should know what I want." The last time all of our needs were met without our having to take any responsibility was in the womb; we were never hungry, never hot or cold, and never alone. From the moment we are born, we have to find imperfect ways of communicating our needs, and then live with the limited capacity or desire of others to respond to those needs. No wonder we cry when we are born.

We know that people who take responsibility for what they want to change make more effective and enduring change than those who do not.[25] For example, residents in nursing homes live longer when given more responsibility for their own care, and patients given responsibility for their own medication use significantly less pain medication while also reporting less pain.[26]

It is not easy to take responsibility for the change we want to see in our lives. Fewer than ten percent of smokers and twenty-five percent of people with diagnosable psychological problems ever seek any kind of help.[27] Externalizing responsibility helps protect us from excessive guilt and self-recrimination and helps us hold onto the hope we need to try again. For example, during the painful ending of a long-term relationship, it is tempting to protect ourselves by blaming the other person and not be very curious about our own role in the breakup. The problem is that wherever you go, there you are. It gets progressively more difficult to blame your ex when you begin to see the same patterns reoccurring in each new relationship. You might ask, "How do I keep finding these people, anyway?"

The trick is to take appropriate responsibility for what you can change without blaming yourself for what is out of your control. As a colleague of mine liked to say, "More curiosity, and less judgment" (A. Redmountain, personal communication, 1998). Some of us have not yet found the courage to take responsibility for what we can change, which is ourselves. We are still preoccupied with blaming others for what is wrong with our lives. For many years, I complained about my wife leaving the sponge in the sink, underneath a pile of dirty dishes. One day we were visiting her parents, and I saw that her mother also left the sponge in the sink. Dismayed, I realized that generations of women in my wife's family had probably been leaving the sponge in the sink. In a moment of uncharacteristic insight, I went to the grocery store and bought several packages of sponges. Every time I could not find a clean sponge, I simply brought out a nice new clean one. This strategy worked well for me because I was immediately relieved of the irritation of hunting for a sponge under a pile of dirty dishes. The irony is that within a few months, my wife not only stopped leaving the sponge in the bottom of the sink, she bought a beautiful sponge holder and began to fuss at me when I did not put the sponge in the holder. I was able to solve the sponge problem as soon as I stopped trying so hard to change my wife, and took responsibility for resolving my own irritation. Paradoxically, my letting go of trying so hard to change my wife seemed to make it easier for her to change.

It is currently fashionable to blame all of our life struggles on genetics or a chemical imbalance. The struggle to lose weight is blamed on genetics, unhappiness is attributed to a chemical imbalance, or alcohol abuse is blamed on the disease of alcoholism. Abraham Lincoln said that a man's face after forty is his own responsibility and Lincoln was an unattractive man. Obviously, Lincoln's inherited genetics had something to do with his appearance, but Lincoln's point was that by the age of forty his accumulated life experiences had more of an effect on his appearance than the genetics he was born with. The emerging field of epigenetics supports Lincoln's point with research suggesting that our ongoing lived experience dictates which aspects of our genetic potential are actuated or inhibited.[28]

Others of us have not yet found the serenity to accept the things we cannot change; we blame ourselves for things outside of our control. I worked with one woman who apologized so frequently for things she had no control over that I teased about fining her a quarter every time she said "I'm sorry." This is more common in women in our culture because we socialize women to minimize the importance of their own needs and focus on meeting the needs of others.

Not blaming ourselves for what we cannot change opens the door to a fuller, more radical acceptance of personal responsibility. I worked with a man named Barry who had a long-standing habit of taking food off his family's plates at the dinner table. Barry's family complained angrily because to them it was emblematic of his general disregard of their personal space. They talked about it many times in family therapy, and Barry promised repeatedly to change this behavior but was never successful. Barry felt awful about his repeated failure to change this simple behavior.

I told Barry he was stuck because he had not yet accepted full responsibility for his behavior, and had not yet committed himself fully to making this change. I suggested to Barry that every time he sat down to eat with his family, that he take a moment to reflect in silent prayer, close his eyes and dedicate himself to not taking food off his family's plates as the single most important priority of that meal. I told Barry that if he made this more important than his own pleasure from eating, more important than conversation with his family, if he made that level of commitment and accepted full responsibility for the behavior, I was certain he would stop. Four months later, Barry reported that he had not once taken any food from his family's plates. His children were now offering him leftover food from their plates, which he declined.

In another example, I worked with a combat veteran named David who had an angry and volatile relationship with his adolescent son. One night, David stayed up late to confront his son who was out long past his curfew. When his son walked in the door, David punched him in the face and knocked him unconscious. When David told me remorsefully about what happened, I asked David if he could tell me with one hundred percent certainty that he would never again be violent with his son. David protested that he had posttraumatic stress disorder and episodes of dissociative rage when he was not even aware of, much less responsible for, his own behavior. I told David that until he could find a way of being fully responsible for his behavior that he could not discipline his son, or interact with him in any way that created any risk of violence. In this case, David was not ready to take full responsibility for his behavior, and so he decided that the only responsible thing to do was to move out of the house until he could be fully responsible for his own behavior.

Some argue that an excessive focus on individual responsibility detracts from our responsibility to work on larger systemic change. Family therapists have long argued that helping individuals change is not as effective as working with the entire family system.[29] On a larger scale, a group of therapists in the 1960s were concerned that psychotherapy should not help people learn to silently adjust to a dysfunctional system, but rather should help people advocate for change in that system.[30]

While these concerns clearly have merit, it is also true that working to change ourselves is one of the most powerful ways to change larger systems. As Gandhi said, "You must be the change you wish to see in the world." For example, the women's movement facilitated radical shifts in individual consciousness that inevitably led to larger changes in families, the workplace, communities, and eventually the entire world.

Every journey begins with a single step. In the journey of personal change and transformation, once you have taken the first step of accepting responsibility for what you can change, and stopped blaming yourself for what you cannot change, then you have already traveled a good part of the way. In fact, once you have taken this first step, change is inevitable.

KNOWING WHAT YOU KNOW

And you will know the truth, and the truth will set you free.

—John 8:32[31]

The final step in embracing experience is validating your experience, knowing what you know. People come to me seeking answers to some of the most important questions of their lives: Why don't my relationships ever work out the way I hope they will? Why can I not achieve the success I believe I deserve? What will it take to make me truly happy? When you go to an expert for help, you expect answers to your questions, but therapists generally do not tell you what to do. Instead, we suggest that the answer to your questions lies within you, and that your job is to know what you already know.

Sounds a bit like a scam, like one of the Zen koans you can never make sense of, like "what is the sound of one hand clapping?" How can I know what I do not already know? If I already knew what I need to know, I would not be asking you.

Chilean biologists Humberto Maturana and Francisco Varela suggest that all living systems are autopoietic, meaning they contain with them everything needed to be self-maintaining. For example, a biological cell contains the nucleic acids and proteins needed to maintain the cell, as opposed to a nonliving system such as factory, which is allopoietic, meaning it needs to import resources continually to sustain it.[32] In this culture, when we are stuck we tend to look for answers outside ourselves, to think of ourselves as allopoietic rather than autopoietic. We do not have a well-developed contemplative tradition to help us have the faith that turning inward and embracing our experience will give us the clarity we seek.

Let's look at Jane's example. Jane is a woman in her mid-fifties who has been married for twenty-seven years and has a son in college and a daughter who is finishing high school. I worked with Jane for quite a while before she began to talk about her marriage in anything more than superficial terms. First, she divulged that her husband had only a minimal relationship with their children, rarely spending any time with them and almost never touching them. Later, Jane began to talk about their sexual relationship, saying that she had not experienced any pleasure sexually with her husband for many years and there were times when even his touch made her recoil.

One night, Jane's husband got so angry that he hit their new puppy hard enough to knock him over the side of the deck. Something clicked in Jane. This last incident helped Jane to know what she had been trying to know for a very long time. Jane eventually filed for divorce, and for months, she swung wildly back and forth between times when she felt strong and clear, confident of knowing her own truth, and moments of abject panic and terror when she lost any confidence in knowing herself. Fortunately, Jane was willing to do the hard work and hang in there long enough to know fully everything that she needed to know, which enabled her to move forward with confidence.

THE TALKING CURE

"Abracadabra," from the ancient Aramaic, meaning to create by speaking.

There are many good techniques for embracing experience. Therapists are particularly enamored with putting experience into words and sharing it with others, a powerful way to embrace experience. In the biblical story of creation, God creates the entire world just through the act of speaking (Rabbi J. Lesser, personal communication, 2006). "And God said, 'Let there be light, and there was light.'"[33]

A young Sigmund Freud named his groundbreaking new treatment "the talking cure" (a title first suggested by his patient, Anna O.) when he found that the process of formulating our experience into words and talking about it with the accompanying emotions is by itself a powerful vehicle for change. I have always wanted to have bumper stickers made up that say "Life is a bitch . . . but talking about it helps." You have to embrace an experience in order to put it into words. You have to reflect on your experience, chew it up, and digest the experience in order to make sense of it. Psychoanalyst Robert Carrere wrote that when he can "find the word or phrase that articulates it (an experience) in a 'just so' way, I slide into the experience with all the richness and depth of feeling and thought of which I am capable."[34]

Extensive psychological research demonstrates the beneficial effects of talking about experience. Brain imaging studies suggest that putting experience into words activates the right ventral prefrontal cortex, which may help suppress activity in the parts of the brain that produce emotional distress.[35] Applied research suggests that people who talk about or even write about their experience are not only happier and report lower emotional distress, but also have improved immune system function and fewer illnesses than those who do not express their experience.[36] Other research confirms that actively avoiding talking about experience compromises immune, cardiac, and vascular systems, as well as the brain and nervous system functioning. Not talking about childhood trauma is correlated with a number of health problems including hypertension, cancer, and influenza.[37]

We seem to have a compelling need to tell our stories. Most religions feature some kind of ritual of confession, and the "stranger on the bus" phenomenon speaks to our strong need to tell our story even to a complete stranger.[38] Clearly, the experience of talking to someone is different from the experience of talking to yourself. In fact, in this culture talking to yourself is generally regarded with some suspicion. We are drawn to tell our stories even when it is painful to do so. In one study, participants were asked to write or talk about deeply personal experiences. Despite the fact that most participants rated the experience as "extremely upsetting" and twenty-five percent of them cried during the experiment, ninety-eight percent said they would do it again.

Early in the process of psychotherapy, people often ask what they should talk about. I encourage people to talk about whatever feels most pressing to them in that moment, to trust that whatever is "in the front of your mind" will be the most helpful thing to talk about, even if you cannot immediately see how it is relevant. All the threads of our experience are woven together, so every thread eventually connects with all of the other threads of your life. Some of the most productive psychotherapy sessions have revolved entirely around following the thread of an off-hand comment made while walking down the hall.

The way we talk about our experience is more important than the content. As with Trying Harder, there are ways to talk that help us to either embrace further or avoid embracing our experience. Talking about our experience facilitates change to the extent that we are able to be present, to embrace fully our experience as we talk about it. In most social situations, it is quite common for people to talk about their experience in a detached way, almost as if they were an observer rather than a participant in their own lives. When we talk in this kind of distant, detached fashion, with no apparent emotion, as if we were talking about something that happened to someone else, we create impasses by reinforcing the separations between our lived experiences and us.

The biblical text of the story of the exodus from Egypt says, "You shall explain to your child on that day, it is because of what the Eternal One did for me when I went free from Egypt."[39] This is not a grammatical error. The text is written this way to encourage readers to tell the story as if they were experiencing it themselves in the present. We accomplish this in psychotherapy by slowing the retelling to a crawl, and encouraging the patient to speak in first person, present tense. The therapist facilitates the process with questions such as "What are you seeing now?" "What do you smell now?" or "Tell me what it would be like for me if I were in your place right now."

You can try this for yourself. The next time you are talking to a friend about something that is important to you, try slowing down enough to pay attention to your experience. Are you engaged in what you are talking about, and engaged with the person you are talking with, or are you just repeating a story you have told before, repeating the same phrases and punch lines? Try slowing down enough to embrace your experience of the moment more fully, and then talk about that experience rather than your story. See if that does not make a difference in how you feel and a difference in your sense of connection with the person you are talking with.

❸

CHANGE THROUGH RELATIONSHIPS

It took a series of relationships to get you into this mess,
And it's going to take a relationship to get you out of it.

—Dick Felder

Relationships are one of the most powerful tools to help us make effective and enduring change in our lives. Multiple studies document the emotional and physical benefits of being in a long-term, committed relationship. Married people live longer than those who are single, and your chances of making a positive health change are much better if your intimate partner is successfully making that same change.[1]

In psychotherapy, the nature of the relationship between patient and therapist is more important than the theoretical orientation of the therapist or any therapeutic technique used.[2] In medicine, the nature of your relationship with your physician has as much or more to do with your getting well than any medication or other treatments prescribed.[3] For example, it is common to find very different results for the same drug given in different settings. In one study, the same antidepressant drug was more than twice as effective in one hospital as it was in another.[4]

On the other hand, the absence of significant relationships is a major risk factor for problems ranging from depression to coronary artery disease,[5] and Alzheimer's disease.[6] People who have greater social networks live longer at a ten-year follow-up.[7] In this chapter, you will learn how to identify and cultivate the kinds of relationships that will help you create the change you want to bring about in your life.

AUTHENTIC OR IMITATIVE?

> When you think you know who someone is, at that moment, you have kept them from growing.
>
> —Native American saying

We know that people do change dramatically throughout the course of significant relationships, whether those relationships are with a friend, intimate partner, teacher, clergy, mentor, or therapist. The question is whether change in relationships is authentic or imitative. Do relationships help us become more fully who we are or make it more difficult to be authentic? Are we most genuinely ourselves when we are alone or in relationship? For example, newly married couples tend to show a "dietary convergence" after they get married, with men tending to eat less meat and more low-fat milk and women eating more snack foods.[8] Are the men learning from their wives and authentically adopting healthier eating habits, or are they simply trying to please their partners or avoid conflict? Are the women sliding down to their partner's less healthy eating habits or being more authentic in their eating now that they are less obsessively focused on finding a mate? As the Sufi judge in chapter 1 said, "They are both right." Change in relationships can be imitative or authentic.

In this culture, we tend to be concerned that change in relationships will be more imitative than authentic. We believe we are most authentically ourselves when we are by ourselves, and worry about relationships overly influencing us, making us lose touch with who we genuinely are, losing the melody of who we are against the harmony of the expectations of others.

Researchers use the term *fundamental attribution error* to describe the tendency in Western cultures to attribute our behavior to enduring personality characteristics, and underestimate the effect of relational and situational variables on our lives.[9] When close friends fall in love and seem greatly changed we worry that they are being unduly influenced, not being themselves. When friends get involved in something new so passionately that it is all they can talk about, we joke that they "drank the Kool-Aid," or uncritically swallowed the values of a group and lost their sense of themselves. When we feel despairing or lost in our intimate partnerships, we think about "getting away" in order to "find ourselves." Men in particular are anxious about being unduly influenced in intimate relationships, and give each other a fair amount of grief whenever they seem to have changed to please a woman, using insults like "pussy whipped" to imply that the man has been dominated by a woman, feminized, or emasculated.[10]

INTRAPSYCHIC AND RELATIONAL MODELS

This fear of loss of self in relationships follows from an underlying intrapsychic rather than relational understanding of human development. In an intrapsychic model, individual needs are the primary driving force in our lives, and relationships are a secondary means of either satisfying or frustrating our individual needs. Freud thought that libido, or psychic energy, was a fixed commodity, meaning the more energy you invest in relationships the less you have available for yourself.[11] Prioritizing the needs of others above one's own needs is pathologized as enmeshed and insufficiently individuated. Psychotherapists love to illustrate this with the analogy of flight attendants instructing passengers that if there is a loss of oxygen they should put on their own oxygen masks before tending to their children.

In an intrapsychic model, healthy development involves a progression from a series of dependent relationships toward increasing self-reliance. Developmental milestones are marked by increasing levels of separation from relationship: weaning, sleeping in your own bed, taking your first steps, potty training, and so on. By the age of four, most kids in this culture have the "false uniqueness syndrome,"[12] valuing themselves for what separates them from others: being taller, smarter, more privileged, faster, or stronger. Seeing ourselves as separate from others and the world makes it easier to act in ways that are less mindful of the impact we have on others and the world. It is easier to hate others if we do not see relationships as interdependent, and easier to pollute our environment if we do not see our interdependence with the planet.

Alternatively, a relational theory of development suggests that relationships, rather than individual needs, are the primary driving force in our lives. In a relational model, connecting with others adds to rather than detracts from the energy available. For example, if you have more than one child, I am sure you loved your first child with all of your heart and did not hold anything back, yet somehow when you had your second child, you uncovered an entirely new storehouse of loving energy to give to that second child you did not even know you had. Similarly, generous people are often puzzled when praised for their giving because they know they are receiving far more than they have ever given.

Mature development, in a relational model, is characterized by the increasing capacity for interdependence and the ability to attend to and value your needs within the context of the needs of others. Rather than thinking of relationships in win-lose terms, a relational model suggests that relationships can only be growth enhancing for one person when they are growth enhancing for both.[13] Carl Jung wrote, "The meeting of two personalities is the like the contact of two chemical substances: if there is any reaction, both are transformed."[14]

Lawrence Kohlberg's well-known research on moral development supported the value of prioritizing one's own needs in relationship (i.e., putting on your own oxygen mask first). Kohlberg's colleague, Carol Gilligan, Ph.D., noticed that he used only male subjects in his research. Gilligan found that women tend to make choices in a relational manner, with their own needs inseparably connected to their awareness and value on the needs of others with whom they are in relationship.[15]

Philosopher Martin Buber wrote that there is no "I" without a "thou," meaning that the very core of who we are is formed in a series of relationships.[16] Early in life, we come to know ourselves, actually come to be ourselves through our relationships with those who care for us. If your mother held you lovingly close when you were born and gazed adoringly into your eyes, then you experienced yourself as lovable and adorable. You had no other reference point. How else could you understand yourself? If, on the other hand, your mother was angry and resentful at the moment of your birth, conflicted about the pregnancy and the changes you would bring to her life, then you probably experienced yourself in a very confusing way as both a blessing and a burden. In the classic Pygmalion effect studies, students whose teachers expected them to be high achievers did better than those students whose teachers did not expect them to do well, regardless of their initial level of ability. It was not just that the teacher's expectations shaped their grading. Those students actually did better when their teacher expected them to; they became who their teacher expected them to be.[17]

Let us look at the process of change in three different kinds of relationships: persuasive relationships in which one person tries to convince the other to change; supportive relationships in which we encourage each other to change; and intimate relationships, which make possible the most profound type of characterological core-level change.

PERSUASIVE RELATIONSHIPS

> Persuasion is often more effectual than force.
>
> —Aesop[18]

> Character may almost be called the most effective means of persuasion.
>
> —Aristotle[19]

In a persuasive relationship, one person tries to convince another to change. The person doing the persuading believes he or she knows what is best for the other person. The target of the interpersonal persuasion, however, may not agree with the persuader's agenda, like the college student resisting his helicopter parent's attempts to micromanage his or her life.

We have all been involved in persuasive relationships, from both sides. All change in relationships is persuasive to some extent, often more than we care to admit. First, our parents, then our peers, and then perhaps an intimate partner are all powerful sources of interpersonal persuasion in our lives.[20] There are a number of professions dedicated to persuading people to change: salespeople attempt to persuade potential customers to buy, leaders try to convince others to follow them, lawyers endeavor to persuade juries to vote their way, and a teacher's job is to persuade students to learn. My own profession of psychotherapy involves a good deal more persuasion than many of us would care to acknowledge.[21] Researchers were disturbed to learn that therapists rated the patients who had moved closer to their own values as more improved than those patients who did not adopt their therapist's values.[22]

Change in a persuasive relationship can be overt, like having an argument with your partner, or trying to convince your boss to give you a raise or get your kids to clean their rooms. In these examples, the change agent's agenda is overt and known by both parties; your partner knows you are trying to get your way, your boss understands that you are trying to get more money, and your kids recognize they are in a power struggle with you. In other cases, the change agent's agenda is covert, like advertisements by political action committees or the brief timeshare presentations that inevitably accompany your "free" weekend getaway.

Developmentally, the natural progression is toward relying less on persuasive relationships and taking increasing responsibility for the change we want to make in our lives. For example, while parents largely set the life agendas for their young children, we expect to work our way out of those persuasive roles as our children take increasing responsibility for their lives. Teachers have a curriculum, a body of information they want to impart, but effective teachers help their students learn rather than trying to teach them. Therapists also inevitably have agendas, sometimes overtly and sometimes covertly, for how we would like to see our patients change. Effective psychotherapy requires letting go of those agendas and empowering patients to create their own change.

Similarly, there are things I have learned through long study and professional experience about the process of change that I would like to teach you. However, my job as an author is not to teach you but to try and help you learn, not to persuade you to follow a formula for change that I have devised, but to empower you to use the information in this book to create your own plan.

What kind of partner should you pick for a persuasive relationship? Because persuasive relationships are inherently hierarchal, any agenda that your partner has, overt or covert, creates the potential for imitative change. It is important to pick someone who listens to and respects your agenda for change, without trying to convert you to an agenda of his or her own, someone who is sufficiently self-reflective to recognize his or her own agendas, not too defensive to acknowledge those agendas, and respects you enough to work toward setting those agendas aside.

SUPPORTIVE RELATIONSHIPS

At times our own light goes out, but is blown again into instant flame by an encounter with another human being.

—Albert Schweitzer

Supportive relationships often involve elements of persuasion, but unlike persuasive relationships, supportive relationships are mutual and nonhierarchal. There are times when we ask someone else to help persuade us to make changes in our lives we have been unable to make ourselves. Examples are hiring a trainer to persuade us to work out or a life coach to persuade us to formulate and stick with a plan for change. We may go to a house of worship, hoping our spiritual leader will inspire and persuade us to change. In one of the most creative weight loss strategies I have ever heard, a good friend of mine who is an ardent Democrat and his friend who is an equally passionate Republican made a weight loss bet together. The friend who did not meet the agreed-upon weight target on a specified date agreed to donate $500 to the other's political party. As you might imagine, they both lost the weight.

Supportive relationships foster change by encouraging us to hang in there and embrace more fully the aspects of our experience we are having difficulty embracing on our own, like the high school teacher who challenged you to dig down deep within yourself and embrace aspects of your potential that you did not even know existed. Supportive relationships facilitate change by helping us penetrate our selective perceptions and denial. It is difficult to pay attention to what we eat, or accurately keep track of our spending. Inviting a supportive partner to help us is one of the most powerful ways to help us know what we know.

Research substantiates that your chances of making a lasting change in your life are greatly increased if you have significant interpersonal support. There are literally hundreds of psychological studies demonstrating the effectiveness of social support networks for people wrestling with life issues ranging from depression[23] to grief[24] to patients with chronic illness and their caregivers[25] to people struggling with a variety of addictions.[26] There is an old Chasidic story about the difference between heaven and hell. In hell, everyone is sitting around a huge banquet table filled with the most sumptuous food imaginable, but they are all starving because everyone has a fork strapped to their hands that is so long that they cannot bring it around to feed themselves. In heaven, the situation is identical, but everyone is well fed because they simply reach across the table and feed each other.

We live in what has been called the age of isolation.[27] We are tribal by nature, and not meant to tolerate high levels of emotional distress alone. The technological changes that have isolated us from our extended families and communities have far outstripped our psychological capacity to keep up with those changes. Social isolation is as big a risk factor for the development of cancer as cigarette smoking.[28] One of the most well-known studies of the impact of peer support found that women who attended a support group for breast cancer patients responded better to treatment and actually lived significantly longer than those patients who did not attend a support group.[29] The author concluded that, based on the research data, for an oncologist not to refer patients to a support group study could be understood as malpractice.

Given the risks of isolation, it makes sense to prescribe supportive relationships and community involvement in the same way we encourage exercising and healthy diet. Imagine if you went to your physician about feeling run down and having recurrent illnesses and your physician asked about the nature of your interpersonal support network. Your physician is not likely to ask you about the health of your relationships, but you could do that for yourself right now.

EXERCISE

Look at table 3.1 "Supportive Relationship Checkup." In the first column, make a list of all of the important relationships in your life, whether the relationship is with one person or a group of people (faith community, neighborhood association, book club, etc.). In the second column, make a note of the last time you had any substantial connection with this person or group. Look over your list and take note of the relationships you are keeping up with and nurturing and those you may be neglecting. Are you investing enough energy in the relationships that are most important to you? Are you investing too much energy in other relationships that are not as important to you? In the third column, write one specific action you will take to invest more in a relationship that is important to you, but you have been neglecting or one specific action you will take to put less energy into a relationship that is not as important to you.

In the fourth column, write something about what you have received from this person or group, and in the fifth column jot down something about what you give to this person or group. Review these last two columns and in the sixth column make a note of any relationship you feel is out of balance, and any relationship in which your giving and receiving are not roughly in balance. So many of the people I work with as a therapist suffer from the effects of isolation, sometimes even when surrounded by other people. They talk about feeling empty and deprived, not having enough, so it is counterintuitive when I suggest that they will not feel better until they start to focus more on giving, and less on what they are not receiving.

This is an exercise you may find helpful to repeat annually, and then review regularly throughout the year.

It is not hard to find people to support your change. Once you declare your intention to change, all kinds of people will come out of the woodwork with advice and offers of help. It is important to choose someone who will help you move further into your experience rather than colluding with you to avoid your experience. This is more likely if the person you choose to support you is already comfortable embracing that same experience himself or herself, or is open to working together with you to embrace more fully that experience.

Allowing ourselves to be more vulnerable in mutually supportive relationships can evoke some of our general discomfort with dependency in relationships. In our culture, we venerate independence, and look down on dependency as a sign of weakness, a dangerous vulnerability. We are a nation of pioneers, hearty souls who settled the west, homesteaders who prided themselves on their self-reliance. When we become ill, we try to manage our affairs so that we will not become "a burden on anyone." When we are in financial trouble, we borrow money from a bank

Table 3.1: Supportive Relationship Checklist

Important Relationships	Last Connection	Commitment to Action	What You Have Received	What You Give	Relationship Balance

because it is a "bad idea to borrow from friends." When we are sad, or in pain, we isolate ourselves, convinced that no one would want to be around anyone who feels the way we do. We create social institutions—Medicare, insurance, social service agencies, and psychotherapy—to protect ourselves from the experience of dependency.[30]

In our culture, we think of independence as a mature state that one achieves by transcending the need for dependency. We believe that infants are completely dependent at birth, and that the parent's job is to socialize them into increasing independence. We mark developmental milestones by the achievement of new levels of independence: walking, potty training, going to school, and so on. These values are so taken for granted in our culture that we assume they are universal. However, in Japan, infants are considered completely independent at birth, and the Japanese believe that it is the parent's job is to socialize children into appropriate social dependency.[31]

An alternative conception is that psychological independence does not supersede the need for emotional dependence, but that true independence is predicated on the capacity for a mature dependency.[32] Independence without the capacity for mature interpersonal dependency can only be self-sufficiency, which is only pseudo independence. From this perspective, the capacities for independence as well as the capacity for dependence are both requirements for a fully supportive relationship.

INTIMATE RELATIONSHIPS

> Each friend represents a world in us, a world possibly not born until they arrive, And it is only by this meeting that a new world is born.
>
> —Anais Nin[33]

> However good or bad you feel about your relationship, the person you are with at this moment is the "right" person, because he or she is the mirror of who you are inside.
>
> —Deepak Chopra[34]

While we have all experienced significant life change in both persuasive and supportive relationships, the most profound life-altering change, change at the core level of who we truly are, is most powerfully accomplished through intimate relationships.

What do I mean by an intimate relationship? Intimacy is, by definition, a relational experience; that is, intimacy implies a relationship with an intimate other. In this culture, we often talk about intimacy as if it were synonymous with sexual intimacy, as in, "we were intimate last night," meaning "we had sex last night." However, we know that not all sexual relationships are intimate, and most intimate relationships are not sexual. In the simplest terms, an intimate relationship is one in which I am able to be more fully myself while also deeply connected with someone else.[35] There is a deeply shared sense of connection as well as an awareness of one's own separateness, an awareness of one's own needs as well as the needs of others.

Intimate relationships intensify the process of change by helping us become aware of and then potentially embrace aspects of ourselves we have not yet integrated. We seem different in various relationships because we truly are different. New aspects of us are evoked in different contexts. There is a Chassidic story about the child of a rabbi who used to wander in the woods. His father asked him, "Why do you go there?" The child replied, "I go there to find God." The father told him it was good to search for God, but reminded him that God is the same everywhere. "I know," replied the child. "But I'm not."

The most powerful example for me was the experience of meeting my wife. When I first met my wife, I had very little interest in kids, I just never thought about them very much. Five days after I met my wife I told a close friend I wanted to have children with her, and now being a father is one of the most important, core aspects of who I am as a person. Where did that come from? Would I have discovered this critical part of myself on my own, or would it have remained dormant, waiting for the right interpersonal context to elicit it?

The process of change through encountering unintegrated aspects of ourselves in relationship is not always so easy or self-affirming. There is a scene in the movie *Gandhi*[36] in which the Hindus and Muslims of India are rioting and Gandhi refuses to eat until the killing stops. A Hindu man bursts into Gandhi's room, and tells him that he has killed a Muslim man and his wife, orphaning their child. The man wants to know what he must do to be forgiven. Weak with hunger, Gandhi tells the man that he must take that child into his home, and raise him as if he were his own. Elated to have a way out, the man starts to leave the room when Gandhi stops him to add, "But you must raise the child as a Muslim."

One of the richest sources of new information about ourselves lies in our critical judgments of others. Shakespeare wrote, "The lady doth protest too much, methinks."[37] Consider the possibility that many of the things that upset you most about your intimate partner are distressing primarily because you have not integrated the aspect of yourself that you see in others. For example, if you are upset about your partner being messy and not putting things back where they belong, perhaps you feel internally chaotic yourself and rely on external organization to soothe yourself internally.

The ability to be intimate, to be yourself in relationships with others, is predicated on having a history of attachments consistent enough to allow the development of a secure sense of self. Some people's early history of relationships is so unreliable that they fail to develop this consistent sense of self. They are "other-centered"; that is, they see themselves primarily through the eyes of others. Their lives are chaotic and traumatic as they are tossed in whichever direction the winds of interpersonal influence are blowing. The person without a secure sense of self may present as highly guarded or defended in order to protect his or her fragile sense of self from what is experienced as the undue influence of others. These are the people we talked about earlier in the chapter who see relationships as a threat to their autonomy, who struggle to hold onto their own experience in the face of the differing experience of others.

The willingness to engage in this process of mutual growth is what makes an intimate relationship mutually enhancing rather than mutually destructive. Because intimate relationships have such great potential to facilitate change, it is particularly important to choose our intimate partners with care. It is even more important to choose someone who does not have his or her own agenda for your change, and is committed to work with you in a mutually growthful experience. Furthermore, it is best to pick someone who either has a greater range of lived experience in the area you want to expand, or who welcomes the opportunity to expand further his or her own experience. This is what a psychotherapist's job is, to come to the therapeutic relationship with a more developed capacity to embrace a wider range of experience (see chapter 7).

PROFESSIONAL HELPING RELATIONSHIPS

> Nothing is more surprising than the rise of the new within ourselves. We do not foresee or observe its growth. The new being is born in us, just when we least believe in it. It appears in remote corners of our souls which we have neglected for a long time. It opens up deep levels of our personality which had been shut out by old decisions and old exclusions. It shows a way where there was no way before. The new which we sought and longed for comes to us in the moment in which we lose hope of ever finding it.
>
> —Paul Tillich[38]

A colleague of mine likes to say that when you are overwhelmed, you need to either lower your expectations or hire more help (P. R. Clance, personal communication, 1994). This advice runs contrary to our strong cultural value on self-reliance. We think of help as something you accept reluctantly, and only when we really "need it," meaning only after we have exhausted all possible means to resolve the situation on our own.

These prejudices are even more pronounced when it comes to seeking professional help for personal problems. Even men who are comfortable asking for directions are reluctant to seek a psychotherapist's help with an important life change. Alternatively, if we could set aside our prejudices about dependency and self-reliance, we might be able to ask instead whether a psychotherapist can help with whatever change we are contemplating in our lives. Research makes it clear that psychotherapy is one of the few areas of healthcare that pays for itself; in other words, every dollar spent on psychotherapy returns more then one dollar in healthcare savings.[39] This should not surprise us because we know that talking about what bothers you with someone who cares improves overall health on a number of measures.

Given this research, it is likely that seeking the assistance of a psychotherapist will help you with whatever life change you are contemplating. We know that change in psychotherapy is a concentrated version of change on your own, so seeking professional help will likely mean that you will change faster and more efficiently, and you are more likely to be able to sustain that change. The decision to seek professional help is more of a cost-benefit question rather than one of absolute necessity. How much help will you receive if you seek professional help and at what cost? What is the cost of not seeking professional help?

4

GETTING STUCK AND UNSTUCK

Nothing is permanent but change.

—Heraclitus[1]

If I had my life to live over I would make all the same mistakes, only sooner.[2]

—Tallulah Bankhead

The surest way to be stuck is to insist on never being stuck. Being stuck is an inevitable part of the process of change. The only way to avoid being stuck is to stay on the surface of your life, like the couple who insists they never argue, all the way to the divorce attorney's office. Change happens not by avoiding impasses but by working through the inevitable impasses you encounter along the way. In this chapter, you will learn about some of the most common ways that people get stuck in the process of change and how to work through those impasses.

SEPARATIONS FROM EXPERIENCE

> The man who is often thinking that it is better to be somewhere else
> than where he is excommunicates himself.
>
> —Henry David Thoreau[3]

If change is the result of embracing experience, it follows that separations from lived experience interfere with the process of change. The
more fully we embrace our experience, the more we change; and the
more separated we become from our experience, the more we are stuck.

While there may be gurus somewhere in India who completely embrace their experience of the moment, the rest of us move in and out
of various levels of embracing our immediate experience, more often
separated from our experience than embracing it. As the pace of our
lives moves faster and faster, it becomes increasingly difficult to stay
connected to our lived experience. Thoreau said, "Cutting wood warms
us twice; once in the cutting and once in the burning."[4] I have had the
experience of cutting five cords of wood for a winter's heat. It is certainly much easier to flip the switch on a thermostat, but there is a layer
of experience lost in that trade. I had a relationship with the cutting and
burning of that wood that I cannot have with a thermostat.

Most of the experiences we require to change are readily available to
us in the world. If we need to learn about emotional generosity, there
are loving people who can teach us and people with genuine needs
who can help us learn. If we need to learn about finiteness and living
responsibly, there are wise people who choose to live with less who can
teach us and people who are suffering from the excesses of their lives
who can help us learn.

Although the experiences we require to change are readily available
to us, what makes change so challenging is that the very experiences we
need most to change are the ones we have the most difficulty embracing. It is experiences that are new to us that most help us change, novel
experiences that have the most potential to challenge the way we see
ourselves and the world we live in. The problem is that it is hard for us
to see what we do not expect to see, hear what we do not expect to hear,
feel what we do not expect to feel, or think what we do not expect to
think. This is *cognitive dissonance,* and it is the underlying mechanism

of prejudice: prejudging experience in ways that interfere with our ability to embrace our lived experience.

Psychologist Sid Jourard wrote:

> We begin life with the world presenting itself as it is. Someone—our parents, teachers, analysts—hypnotize us to "see" the world and construe it in the "right" way. These others label the world, attach names and give voices to the being and events in it, so that, thereafter, we cannot read the world in any other language or hear it saying other things to us. The task is to break the hypnotic spell, so that we become undeaf, unblind and multilingual, thereby letting the world speak to us in a new voice and write all its possible meanings in the book of our existence.[5]

To compound matters further, the more stressed you are, the more difficult it is to take in novel experiences, which means that it is most difficult to change when you are most stressed and most need to change.[6] For example, if you are not feeling very confident at work, hearing your boss compliment you in front of the whole staff is just what you need to build your confidence. The problem is that the more worried you are about what he is going to say, the more likely you are either to not hear those compliments or to discount them by telling yourself that your boss says that about everyone or he just has not yet figured out what a bad job you are doing.

This resistance to the very experiences we most need to change is visible on a neurobiological level. While we think of our nervous system as primarily receptive, bringing in information about the world, we actually have ten times as many nerve fibers carrying information downstream from our brain to our sense organs as there are nerve fibers going upstream from the sense organs to the brain.[7] This means that the potential experience of hearing your boss sing your praises has to battle upstream against the 10:1 current of your deeply held conviction that you are not doing a good job. Your boss approaches you to congratulate you after the meeting and does not understand why you nervously avoid him.

In this chapter we will talk about understanding impasses in relational, rather than intrapsychic, terms, and we will look at three ways that people get stuck by becoming separated from their experience: habits, mistaking derivatives of experience for lived experience, and trauma.

IS IT YOU OR IS IT ME . . . OR IS IT US?

> Women hope men will change after marriage, but they don't; men
> hope women won't change, but they do.
>
> —Bettina Arndt[8]

When we feel stuck in our lives, we tend to either blame others or find
the fault within ourselves. However, as we discussed in the previous
chapter, the answer is actually more complex; it is not *you* or *me*; it is
us. The impasses in our lives are relational; they are about where we are
stuck in the relationships in our lives.

This is not how most people think about relationships. Most couples
come to my office with the not-so-hidden agenda of getting me to fix
their partner. They are pretty well convinced that their happiness is
dependent on their partner changing certain behavior patterns. For example, she thinks he needs to work less or he thinks she needs to spend
less money. He thinks she needs to be supportive of him or she thinks he
needs to be more involved with the kids. It is difficult for either of them
to see how interdependent their complaints are. For every partner who
overworks, there is someone covering for him and over-accommodating.
For every partner who spends too much, there is someone who keeps
paying the bills and does not set limits. For every partner who is not
supportive, there is someone playing the role of self-reliant martyr; and
for every partner who is not involved with his children, there is someone
who does not expect much of him or trust him with the children.

I think about relationships as a dance. When two people meet, each
of us invites the other to dance in the way that is most familiar to us,
the way we learned to dance in our families growing up. Consciously,
we try to pick someone who dances in a complementary way. If I am
self-critical, I seek a partner who appears to be endlessly supportive and
reassuring. If I am accustomed to being the caretaker in my family, I will
consciously seek out a partner who is more self-reliant.

This all makes sense on a conscious level, but in intimate relationships
it is our unconscious that actually drives the ship. Although we consciously look for a partner to play a complementary role, unconsciously
we pick partners who challenge us, partners with the potential to help us
grow and change. For example, if I am self-critical, I will find a partner

who loves me but is less than effusive in her praise, forcing me to learn how to soothe my own anxieties.

EXERCISE

Here is a brief exercise to see how this works in your own life. If you are in an intimate relationship now, make a list of some of your partner's shortcomings, the things about your partner that you habitually complain about and often find yourself wishing were different. If you are not currently in an intimate relationship, pick any previous significant relationship.

Now think back through some of the significant relationships from your past. You will probably recall a relationship with someone who had all of the desirable characteristics you complain your partner does not. So what happened? Did you pick the wrong person? Odds are that if you reflect back on that earlier relationship you will find that it did not work because there was no spark, no chemistry between the two of you.

I grew up in a very narcissistic family, and approval from my parents was contingent upon my accomplishments. I only felt good about myself when I was living up to my parent's expectations of me. For the first ten years of my marriage, I tried mightily to get my wife to do this dance with me. I relied heavily on my wife to meet my narcissistic needs and prop up my self-worth. Every day I brought my latest accomplishments to her like a cat dragging in its latest kill to put at the feet of his owner, hoping against hope that I would get the praise I so desperately believed I needed. My wife was remarkably and almost uniformly unimpressed. Occasionally I would get a little nod to tide me over to the next oasis, but she was generally unimpressed. I used to joke that if I won a Nobel Prize my wife would smile benignly at me and then start talking about whatever family issues needed our attention.

I was devastated by this lack of narcissistic feeding. We fought long and hard about it, I frequently blamed my wife for the internal emptiness and lack of fulfillment I often felt, and there were times when I was certain I had chosen the wrong partner. After being stuck in this painful impasse together for a very long time, something unexpected happened. My wife still does not give me a lot of praise for my accomplishments in the world, but I started to notice that she is generous with her love and support of me for being a warm and loving person. She loves me when I get it right with the kids or open my heart to someone in need. In other words, she loves me when I act like a *mensch,* and the more she loves me for being a mensch, the more I feel like a mensch, and the more I feel like a mensch, the more I act like a mensch. I still cannot get her to ask me about my golf game, but instead of that hurting my feelings, it just makes me smile because I know where the good stuff is and how to get it.

HABITS

A foolish consistency is the hobgoblin of little minds.

—Ralph Waldo Emerson[9]

If you have always done it that way, it's probably wrong.

—Charles Kettering[10]

Habit is habit, and not to be flung out of the window by any man, but coaxed downstairs a step at a time.

—Mark Twain[11]

A little girl was watching her mother prepare dinner, and noticed that her mother sliced the end off the roast before placing it in the pan. The girl asked her mother why she did it that way, and her mother said, "I don't know. My mother always did it that way, and so I do too. Let's call her and ask her."

They called the grandmother and asked the same question, and she said, "I don't know, *my* mother always did it that way and so I do too. Let's go see your great-grandmother and ask her about it."

They all got in the car and went to see the little girl's great-grand-mother. When they put the question to her, the old woman laughed aloud, reached into a kitchen cabinet and pulled out a very old, small roasting pan. She told them, "*My* mother only had this one small roast-ing pan, and when she bought a roast it often wouldn't fit into the pan, so she had to cut the end off."

Habits are an inevitable part of life. They not only help us to live more efficiently, they are comforting as well. Most of us follow a consistent pattern in our morning ritual: bathing, dressing, and eating in a particular order. There is a long-forgotten rationale for this sequence, but we do not consider the problem anew each morning, reevaluating the most efficient sequence or gauging our internal readiness to bathe, dress, or eat. It might be more authentic to reconsider the sequence of our morning tasks each day; on the other hand, we might never get to work on time.

Although habits are essential, they become problematic to the extent that they separate us from our lived experience. We come to experience the world in certain habitual ways, which then limit the ways we can experience the world. The solid line in the middle of table 4.1 ("A") graphically represents the fluctuations of experience in our daily lives. Sometimes the line moves one way, sometimes another, but the line is rarely flat for long because experience is dynamic, always changing. Any line that is relatively flat and does not shift with the changing circumstances of life represents a habit. The gray line at the top of the table ("B") represents someone with a habitually anxious style, someone who is anxious regardless of the circumstances. This person is anxious in situations that have been problematic for him or her in the past, and anxious in situations that have never been difficult. He or she is anxious in situations where others are also anxious and anxious when few others feel anxious. He or she responds primarily to habitual anxiety, and is only secondarily responsive to the changing circumstances of life. Conversely, the gray line at the bottom of the table ("C") represents someone with a depressed style, someone who is habitually depressed regardless of the circumstances.

In the same sense, people with an addiction engage in habitual patterns of substance use, largely disregarding the changing environment. When someone asks me if I think he or she is an alcoholic or has an addiction, I suggest that the question of "problematic use" is more meaningful. Problematic use is any habitual pattern of experience that restricts your capacity to experience life more fully and compromises your quality of life. For example, the person who has a cocktail at 5:00 p.m. daily is unlikely to think of himself or herself as an alcoholic because he or she never drinks before 5:00 and rarely has more than that one Scotch. However, having even one drink at 5:00 p.m. every day can

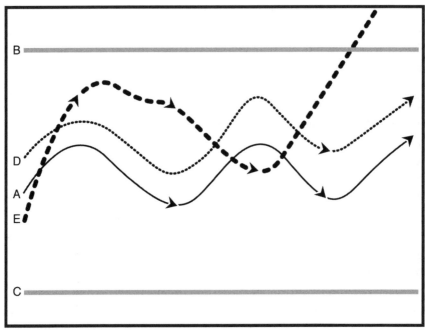

4.1 Habitual Styles

be problematic if it creates separations between you and the ongoing experience of your life, such as avoiding any evening social event where alcohol is not available, or telling your son to wait to play catch until you finish your drink. Even watching the news every night at 6:00 p.m. can be problematic if your husband greets you at the door at 5:55 with a bottle of wine and says that he has arranged for the kids to play next door so that you can have some private time together and you ask him to wait until after the news.

If the relatively flat lines on the chart represent habitual separations from lived experience, then perhaps the dotted line ("D") represents an emotionally healthy person, someone who is maximally responsive to the changing contingencies of life. On the contrary, this line represents an "other-centered" person, someone with an underdeveloped sense of self who sees himself or herself largely through the eyes of others. The other-centered person studies you closely in an effort to make himself or herself into the person you want him or her to be. This person complains that he or she cannot be happy when you are sad, and has no opinion about where to go for dinner.

If it is not healthy to live bound by our habits, or to be overly responsive to the circumstances of our lives, what is a healthy person to do? The dashed line ("E") represents optimal psychological health. Healthy people are not overly restricted by habits. They are responsive to the needs and expectations of others, but retain a core sense of their own experience. They can be intimate, embracing their own experience fully while also attending to the experience of others.

One of the best ways to stimulate change and revitalize your life is to periodically experiment with suspending some of the habits in your life. In French, the word for "experiment" and "experience" are the same.[12] Experimenting with suspending a habit creates new opportunities to embrace your experience more fully. Suspending a habit is not a test of your will power; it is just an experiment to help you learn more about yourself, and you cannot fail an experiment. I am suggesting an experiment, not an attempt to "break" a habit, because attempting to break a habit is just going to war with yourself, and when you go to war with yourself all the casualties are on your side. For example, if you want to know if your drinking is a problem, try experimenting with not drinking for thirty days and pay attention to your experience. If you want to know if watching television is a problem, experiment with unplugging it for thirty days and pay attention to your experience. The more resistant and anxious you are about suspending a particular habit, the more likely it is that your habit is a problem.

At the end of the thirty days, you will have a lot more information about the role this habit plays in your life, and then you will have the opportunity to make some fresh choices about the role you want this habit to play in your life. For example, you may find that your life has not changed considerably after thirty days of not drinking, that you do not miss it much, and your ability to embrace your experience fully is not greatly impacted by your use of alcohol. In this case, you may conclude that your use of alcohol is not habitual and decide to continue your current relationship with alcohol. On the other hand, if after you have turned off the television for thirty days you find your relationship with your kids is noticeably improved and your sexual relationship with your wife is reenergized, you may conclude that your television watching habits are problematic. You may decide to stop watching altogether, or try a new experiment of watching less often to see what more you can learn.

I worked with a single mother who drank two to three glasses of wine every evening. She had a nagging sense that the pattern was both habitual and problematic and avoided bringing it up in her therapy. When she did bring it up, she was surprised at the strength of her resistance to the idea of experimenting with a brief period of abstinence. That degree of resistance gave her enough concern to experiment with suspending this habit. She was surprised at how difficult it was to stop drinking, even for thirty days. Suspending this habit allowed her to see what she could not see before, which was the rippling effects of this problematic use in every aspect of her life, from her job to her relationships with her family and friends. Given what she learned about the pervasive negative impact of her habit, she decided not to resume her drinking, and has been sober now for many years.

One version of experimenting with suspending habits I enjoy is "shuffling the deck." I like to take time to reflect, often during a long car ride or walk on the beach, and take a fresh look at each piece of my life. I look at each piece and imagine what it would be like if I changed that part of my life. What would it be like if I did not live where I live, or had a different job, or sold everything and took off around the world on a sailboat? Most of the times, I end up putting the pieces back in about the same order I had them in before. Even then, this experiment brings a renewed sense of vitality and engagement in my life. Even if I do not make any visible changes, it feels good to know that I have things pretty much the way I want them.

Suspending habits makes sense on a neurological level. The more frequently you respond to a situation in the same way, the more neuronal connections you build between that situation and your response. To change those habits you have to act differently to create new neuronal pathways. You have to "act as if"[13] you are already capable of the change you want to create.

For example, let us say that you want to learn to take better care of yourself by eating better, exercising more, and getting more sleep. Every time you wake up in the morning and think about going to the gym, but roll over and go back to sleep, you are actually building additional neuronal connections between your experience of being tired and the behavior of going back to sleep. You are teaching yourself that the behavior of going back to sleep is an effective response to fatigue. To get

to the gym consistently, you have to forge an entirely new neuronal connection between your experience of fatigue and the behavior of going
to the gym. If you do manage to get up and go to the gym on Monday,
when you wake up on Tuesday the neuronal connections between fatigue and going back to sleep are still going to be much stronger than
the slender new thread you have built for going to the gym. Going to the
gym is likely to feel forced and unnatural. You will have to Try Harder
to reinforce these new internal connections in your brain. Eventually, if
you hang in there long enough, you can establish a stronger neurological connection for going to the gym, and after a while, that becomes a
new habit.

DERIVATIVES OF EXPERIENCE

> The only man I know who behaves sensibly is my tailor; he takes my
> measurements anew each time he sees me. The rest go on with their
> old measurements and expect me to fit them.
>
> —George Bernard Shaw[14]

Another frequent cause of impasses is confusing derivatives of experience with our actual lived experience. Derivatives are meta-experiences,
abstractions that are one step removed from our lived experience. They
are the narratives we construct about our lives, like the stories about
our childhood we have heard so many times, we do not know if we are
remembering an actual experience or just repeating a story. The more
lost we become in derivatives, the more we become characters in a play
of our own creation, and lose our capacity for authentic living. We may
gradually lose the capacity to see ourselves as who we actually are.

Embracing experience inevitably leads to change because experience
is inherently dynamic and flowing. Derivatives, on the other hand, are
abstractions from lived experience. They are stagnant and have no natural flow. Focusing on derivatives results in impasses because it takes us
out of the current of our lived experience.

Basketball coaches tell their players to focus on the mid-section of the
player they are guarding because a player can fool you with a ball fake
or a head fake, but he can't make his middle go one way and his body

the other. Our lived experience is the mid-section to focus on to keep us from being faked out.

Lived experiences are not inherently harmful to us. It is the derivatives we create that are potentially harmful, not the lived experience itself. There is an old saying that pain is mandatory, but suffering is optional. The experience of pain is an inevitable part of living, but suffering is the result of the judgments we make about our experience of pain. It may seem that some experiences are so painful as to inevitably produce suffering, yet Viktor Frankl found great meaning in the midst of his experience of terrible pain during the Holocaust.[15]

For example, Betty talked about calling her parents to share some exciting news. She was disappointed and hurt when her parents did not respond with the enthusiasm she hoped for. When asked to describe her experience of the phone call, Betty scrunched up her face, looked down and said, "Hurt." I asked her if there was more. Betty said that there were many other voices in her head, and I asked her to speak them aloud. She replied, "You are such a big baby, what's the big deal, you are an empty pit and you'll never get enough to satisfy you." I pointed out that these thoughts were derivatives, not her lived experience. These derivatives were a defense against the experience of being hurt because Betty convinced herself that she could not tolerate the experience of feeling hurt. I suggested to Betty that this additional piling on was what was potentially damaging to her, not the experience of being hurt itself.

I knew Betty was a huge Chicago Cubs fan. I reminded her that not only had the Cubs not won the World Series in over one hundred years, but that every time it seemed like they might finally win it all, they seemed to find a way to sabotage the whole thing. Talk about feeling hurt and disappointment! Being a Cub's fan is almost a guarantee to have those feelings in spades! Yet people line up years in advance to buy seasons tickets in order to have the opportunity to feel hurt and disappointment yet again. They take that risk because it makes them feel alive to risk and even to feel the hurt. I suggested that she, too, as a good Cub's fan might be able to tolerate risking the hurt and disappointment she sometimes experiences with her parents, if it was balanced by her love and loyalty to her family and her hope that next year will be better.

Predictions

> The past is just in our memory and the future is just in our imagination, Nothing more than a vision.

> —The Dalai Lama[16]

One of the most common derivatives of experience is the predictions we make about our experience. Embracing experience involves an intense focus on your moment-to-moment experience, as you live it. Considerations of past and future fade from our awareness. You cannot directly experience the past; you can only remember it. You cannot directly experience the future; you can only imagine it.

Predictions shut down the process of change by substituting a false certainty about the future for openness to the present. In reality, it is quite difficult to live in the present, continually embracing our experience of the moment. Quite often, we get out ahead of ourselves and confuse our predictions with our actual lived experience. For example, some people who have been involved in a series of unsatisfying relationships begin to predict with varying degrees of certainty and even obstinacy that they will never meet someone special with whom to share their lives.

Being caught up in predictions about the future is pretty much guaranteed to frighten you, and one of the best ways to calm your fears is to simply sit quietly, breathe deeply, and focus on your experience in the present moment. Horror movies scare us by focusing on what might happen next more than what is happening now. I think that *Psycho* is a more frightening film than *Jaws* because, although there is no violence or gore directly depicted in *Psycho*, our predictions about what might happen next are more terrifying than the graphic violence in *Jaws*.

The simplest problem with predictions is their relative accuracy. Some people are overly optimistic in their predictions while others are overly pessimistic. Research suggests that the majority of people overestimate the likelihood of positive experiences happening to them, and believe that bad things are more likely to happen to other people.[17] When bad things do happen, they rationalize them as anomalies, preserving their optimistic outlook. Other people tend to be overly pessimistic in their predictions. Mark Twain said that ninety percent of what we worry about never happens. That is true, because not only do most of the bad things we worry about never happen, but also because most of the truly awful things that do happen are completely unexpected.

The biggest problem with predictions, however, is not their relative accuracy but rather the false certainty of any prediction. Predictions limit our capacity for future experience in the same way that all of those nerve fibers coming downstream from the brain limit our ability to embrace new experience. I am often amused by the sometimes excruciatingly specific list of characteristics people describe seeking in a life partner. The more they hold onto those predictions, the longer it will take them to find a partner. For this reason, while "I don't know" or "I'm confused" can be unsettling, they are also great harbingers of change.

Judgments

Life is what happens to you while you're busy making other plans.

—John Lennon[18]

Another common derivative is confusing judgments about experience with our lived experience. Young children change so rapidly because they embrace their lived experience with so few judgments. When children are unhappy they cry without inhibition because they do not judge themselves for crying. Children fuss when they cannot get what they want, and they keep fussing until you finally figure it out because no one has taught them yet that they should not be a bother.

Judgments create impasses because they separate us from our ongoing lived experience; they are a defense against embracing aspects of our experience. Although it is uncomfortable to live with the self-judgment that you cannot do something, the false certainty of that judgment can seem easier than facing up to your fears about not living up to your own expectations. It creates a lot of interpersonal tension to judge your partner for not doing what you think he or she should be doing, but that tension might seem easier than looking at our own part in the power struggle and the extent of our dependency on our partner. Judgments like "I can't do that" interfere with our ability to do our best. The judgment "I'm fat" interferes with embracing the full range of feelings we have about our bodies and our struggles to be both consistent and compassionate in our self-care.

Our critical judgments about ourselves are often reflected in the language we use in speaking about ourselves. Our words reflect not only how we feel about ourselves, they can also powerfully shape how we see ourselves, so that over time we come to believe our own self-critical labels. Early in life, significant caretakers may have told us we were stupid. Depending on the level of psychic assault and the extent of emotional resources available us at that time, we may internalize those critical voices and come to adopt them as our own. Psychiatrist Silvano Arietti went so far to suggest that audio hallucinations are nothing more than a concretization of these internalized critical voices.[19]

I interrupt patients whenever I hear them make critical judgments about themselves. I do not interrupt to argue or correct, just to clarify that what they are saying is a judgment, a derivative rather than a lived experience. I say something like, "You cannot have an experience of yourself as stupid because stupid is a judgment, not an experience. Calling yourself stupid is a judgment about whatever experience you were just having, and I wonder if we could talk about the experience you were having right before you started to judge yourself as stupid."

There are also the judgments we make about others, like "you don't care about me," that interfere with embracing our experience of having our feelings hurt when someone does not act the way we hoped he or she would. The judgment "you were wrong to do that" interferes with embracing our experience of understanding how someone else experiences the world differently than we do.

Our judgments of others are often disguised as statements of experience, as in, "I feel like you don't like me." We all know that we cannot speak with authority about another's experience, yet most interpersonal impasses are the result of trying to tell someone about his or her experience rather than attending to our own. If I stick to talking about my own experience I might say, "I'm afraid that you don't like me."

Therapists are guilty of this error when we make interpretations. Telling a patient, "I think your silence is withholding, and indicates resistance to the therapeutic process," versus saying, "When you are silent for long periods of time I get uncomfortable because I do not know what is going on with you. I'm confused as to how I can be most helpful, because I don't know if this is a productive silence, or if you are stuck and could use some help."[20] We keep forgetting that most people are resistant when you try to tell them about themselves, but you encounter a lot less resistance when you speak about your own experience. People don't resist change, they resist being changed.

Recognizing the judgments in our lives, and then setting those judgments aside to allow ourselves to embrace more fully our lived experience is a powerful tool for change. Judgments cut off helpful dialogue, within us and with others. Suspending judgments makes room for fuller dialogue that can enrich our lives. For example, I worked with Bill and Jane, a couple who had long-standing sexual difficulties. Bill looked back on their early sexual experiences as very exciting and emotionally satisfying and wanted very much to get back to the way things used to be. Jane surprised Bill by saying that their early sexual experiences had not been good for her at all, that she had just pretended to enjoy herself but actually felt disconnected and bad about herself. As we continued talking, Jane disclosed that she had been date-raped as a freshman in college. Jane blamed herself for the rape, judging herself for being too flirtatious, too sexual with the young man she was dating. Over time, those judgments increasingly interfered with her ability to embrace her experience of her own sexuality. As Jane continued to work on being aware of and setting aside these critical self-judgments, it freed her up to increasingly embrace her own unencumbered sexual experience in the present with Bill.

TRAUMA

> What cannot be talked about cannot be put to rest, and if not,
> The wounds continue to fester from generation to generation.
>
> —Bruno Bettleheim[21]

Most impasses occur over time, the result of gradual separations from experience. The most damaging and enduring impasses, however, are the result of trauma. If you expose a rat to painful electric shock, the rat will avoid that area of the cage until he forgets his fear. However, if the initial shock is strong enough, the rat may never approach that area of the cage again for the rest of his life.[22]

We all have a set of core beliefs about ourselves, about our relationships, and about the world we live in. For most of us, those beliefs are relatively benign. We believe that we are essentially good people, that others' intent toward us is generally benevolent, that the world is primarily a safe place, and that bad things do not happen to good people.[23] These beliefs are an amalgamation of our lived experience. They are, for the most part, necessary and adaptive. It would be very difficult to drive to work every day if you were thinking about how many people had died in accidents on the road you travel.

We all have experiences that challenge and even threaten these core beliefs. In most cases, we are able to adapt our core beliefs and go on with our lives. For example, if a drunk driver runs a red light and narrowly misses crippling or even killing you, it threatens your naïve belief that the world is safe and bad things do not happen to good people. Being the adaptive, resilient person that you are, you are likely to modify those beliefs. You may conclude that the world is still generally safe, and by in large bad things will not happen to you because you are a good person, but operating a motor vehicle requires an extraordinary level of caution and vigilance. If, however, that drunk driver slams into the other side of your car and kills your wife and young child, then your core beliefs about yourself and the world you live in may be shattered. You may no longer believe that any part of the world is safe or that you are protected from harm because you are a good person. These new trauma-induced beliefs overwhelm your resilience and your capacity to adapt. It makes no sense for you to risk getting back in a car or put yourself in any kind of harm's way again, effectively cutting you off from the very experiences you need to recover.[24]

This is the challenge that confronted theologians following World War II. If God is omniscient and omnipotent, then God was responsible for the murder of nine million people during the Holocaust. Many theologians found their pretrauma core beliefs about God no longer viable. They adapted those core beliefs and developed a post-Holocaust understanding of a God who created the universe and then gave human beings free will to do good or evil.[25] While interred in Auschwitz, Elie Wiesel witnessed a group of Jews put God on trial for abandoning his people and allowing them to be murdered by the Nazis.[26] They found God guilty as charged. How could they do otherwise? Rather than sentencing God for this heinous crime, they decided that the most helpful thing to do was to pray for God.[27]

Trauma functions in the same way as the circuit breakers in your house. If too much current tries to enter your house, the circuit breaker opens, interrupting the flow of current before major damage can happen. Psychically, it is adaptive to use dissociative defenses to create abrupt and extreme separations from experiences whose full impact would likely do damage. The problem is that it is much easier to interrupt the circuit than it is to reconnect the circuit once the danger has passed. The same mechanisms that once served to protect also prevent us from embracing potentially healing experiences.

In this way, trauma is the "gift that keeps on giving." People who are traumatized want to distance, consciously and unconsciously, from the traumatic event and "get back to normal"; in other words, they want to get back to the way they experienced the world prior to the trauma. Unfortunately, this is just not possible. There is no going back in life, no do-overs.

Larger groups seek to protect themselves from the impact of trauma by containing it within traumatized individuals. For example, whenever a group of people hears of someone's cancer diagnosis, you can bet that within minutes someone is bound to ask if that person is a smoker. This question is an attempt to preserve our naïve belief that bad things do not happen to good people (i.e., none of us are going to get cancer because we do not smoke).

Psychiatrist Robert Lifton calls those who have been traumatized the "bearers of forbidden knowledge" because they have learned things about themselves and the world we live in that none of us want to know.[28] Our nontraumatized beliefs that the world is safe and bad things do not happen to good people are remarkably naïve. For example, fifty thousand people die each year in this country in motor vehicle accidents, as many people as died during the entire Vietnam War. Most of those deaths were random; they had nothing to do with whether the driver was being a good person.

There is no better example of this than the tragedy of the Vietnam War. On one level, soldiers in Vietnam were painfully aware that they did not have the support of their larger community, that they were blamed and pathologized by the American people. In addition, soldiers generally served twelve-month tours of duty, which were designed to keep the stresses of combat, as well as the political dissent back home, to a minimum. Paradoxically, it had the opposite effect. Combat is inherently an emotionally devastating experience. It is tolerable only if I believe that the acts I am committing are in the service of a greater good, if I believe there is an overriding cause that justifies my actions. By limiting the tours of duty, we unintentionally created a situation in which individual survival was the goal, and it is psychologically and morally intolerable to do the things required of any good soldier in the service of only his or her own survival.

When a community shares the load of a traumatic experience, it is almost as if some of the psychological burden is lifted from the sufferer and dispersed among the larger community. For example, it is traditional during the Jewish worship service to say a prayer of mourning, and those who have recently lost a loved one or are marking the anniversary of a loss are asked to stand and say this prayer. In some synagogues, the mourners stand alone during the first part of the prayer, and then the entire congregation rises in solidarity with them, praying for their loss as well as those who have no one to mourn for them, specifically those who died during the Holocaust. Imagine the feeling of having an entire community rise and shoulder your grief with you side by side.

Psychotherapy as a profession exists in large part due to the failure of our culture and our families to make room for the telling of our stories. This places the therapist in the unpopular role of bearing witness to stories that the community does not want to hear, and may even actively seek to exclude. Those who speak truths that others do not want to hear often become scapegoated, like the little boy in "The Emperor's New Clothes."[29] The boy's father rebukes him for speaking the truth, protecting the denial of the community against the truth spoken by his son.

The Chinese symbol for "crisis" has two characters: the character for "danger" and the character for "hidden opportunity." To integrate traumatic experience is to be profoundly changed. You may be wounded by your experience, but you also have the opportunity to grow "strong in the broken places."[30] If you embrace experience fully, it is too powerful not to change you. There are Cyprus trees that grow on the cliffs overlooking the Pacific ocean in Monterey, California. Over the years, these trees have become gnarled and twisted, shaped by the pressure of the oceans winds. You might think of those trees as damaged, yet people come from around the world to see their unique beauty.

5

HANGING IN THERE

God must have wanted human beings to be changers,
Else God wouldn't have put that awful unrest in us.

—Alice Walker

When you are going through hell, keep going.

—Winston Churchill[1]

We have previously talked about the separations from lived experience that create impasses in our lives, the places we get stuck and it is difficult to change. These separations from experience are inevitable, and accumulate over time. Like the hard drive in a computer, our accumulated experiences increasingly interfere with our capacity to embrace the experiences we most need to keep us alive and vital. In order to respond flexibly and adaptively to the changing circumstances of the world around us, to continue to grow and mature as a person, we have to challenge ourselves to hang in there and embrace the difficult experiences that help us change.

It is difficult to hang in there and embrace the aspects of your experience that have the most potential for change. After all, you have been avoiding these parts of your experience for a reason. Paying attention to the parts of your experiences you have been avoiding is bound to stir up internal tension. If you avoid the scale so that you do not see your steady weight gain, it is going to generate significant internal tension to weigh yourself. If you avoid paying attention to your partner's drinking, it is going to create a lot of tension when you start paying more attention. If you avoid going through your credit card bills because you do not want to come to terms with your over-spending, it is going to create a lot of internal tension when you start looking carefully at your bills. Things actually do get worse before they get better.[2]

It is natural to want to minimize the tension and internal discomfort in our lives, to seek pleasure and avoid pain. As a result, life can become a series of compromises and adaptations. We do what we need to do to avoid discomfort and disequilibrium. We go along to get along, with ourselves and with others. We come to see the world as we hope it will be, and learn to overlook aspects of our experience that have the potential to challenge our expectations.

These restrictions in awareness are conscious and intentional at first, but they become increasingly automatic, and outside of our awareness. This is an adaptive process to the extent that it modulates our internal distress and allows us to function more effectively in the world. On the other hand, internal tension is the fuel that drives the process of change. Too much internal tension is paralyzing, but too little tension is equally problematic, and is more likely to create stagnation than change.[3] No one has ever come to my office saying, "My life is going pretty well right now, I'm not really in any kind of distress, but I thought I would come in and spend a lot of time and money just to get a look under the hood and make sure everything is O.K." People change when they are in crisis, when the tension they are experiencing from not changing outweighs the tension they anticipate from changing.

TOLERATING INTERNAL TENSION

The truth is that our finest moments are most likely to occur when we are feeling deeply uncomfortable, unhappy or unfulfilled. For it is only in such moments, propelled by our discomfort, that we are likely to step out of our ruts and start searching for different ways or truer answers.

—M. Scott Peck[4]

Freud suggested that early in life we are governed primarily by the pleasure principle, the need to satisfy certain innate biological and psychological needs.[5] Our biological needs include hunger, physical comfort, and rest, but our psychological needs are equally vital. In one well-known study, infants in an orphanage were dying at an alarming rate even though all of their physical needs were well tended to. The babies stopped dying when the nurses started to pick them up and hold them.[6]

Infants and young children have little tolerance for not having their needs met. When they are hungry, tired, or in pain they let us know about it, and they keep letting us know until we figure out what they need. As babies grow and mature psychologically, the raw expressions of the *pleasure principle* are increasingly modulated by the developing *reality principle*,[7] which is our ability to mediate between our physical and emotional needs the reality of the world around us. Our increasing capacity to tolerate internal tension allows us to be more successful in the world by delaying the gratification of short-term needs in the interest of longer-term overarching goals. This allows us to participate effectively in relationships by integrating our own needs with awareness and valuing of the needs of others.

ACTING OUT INTERNAL TENSION

To do nothing is sometimes a good remedy.

—Hippocrates[8]

Tolerating internal tension is the part of the process of change where we most often get into trouble. As our level of internal tension builds and it seems that things are getting worse rather than better, it is natural to want to do whatever we can think of to relieve that tension. The temptation is to do something to discharge the tension by acting it out rather than embracing whatever experience is generating the tension.

Alcohol, staying busy, and consumerism are some of our preferred ways to act out rather than embrace internal tension. For example, I may experience internal tension on the weekends and during my vacations, whenever I slow down enough to notice how distant and estranged I feel from my family. I could act out that tension by bringing more work home or drinking whenever I am home, or I could hang in there and allow myself to embrace more fully the experience of feeling estranged from my family. If I am willing to hang in there long enough to more fully embrace the underlying tension, I am more likely to change my relationship with my family.

The problem with acting out is that it works. Acting out is an effective way to discharge internal tension; it provides an immediate sense of relief, which is why it is so compelling. I worked in an adolescent substance abuse program early in my career, and at every public talk, one parent would inevitably ask, "Why do kids use drugs?" My seemingly facetious, but perfectly serious reply was, "Because they work." (I actually would have liked to say, "For the same reasons you do: they work."). People use alcohol and other drugs because they are unhappy with some aspect of their experience, and they see alcohol and other drugs as a shortcut to feeling differently.

The good news is that acting out works; the bad news is that it does not work for long because, as the old saying goes, wherever you go, there you are. One of the cofounders of Alcoholics Anonymous, Bill W., contacted Carl Jung when he suffered a terrible relapse several years after the conclusion of a successful analysis. Pointing out that the Latin word for alcohol is *spiritus,* Jung suggested that Bill's drinking was acting out his underlying spiritual emptiness, and unless he underwent a profound spiritual transformation, further analysis would be of no further help.

Hanging in there, tolerating internal tension and avoiding the temptation to act out, are not values we support in this culture. We are generally intolerant of internal tension, and think of it as a problem to solve, an unwelcome guest to banish or at least silence. For example, an article in *Woman's Day* magazine exhorted readers to "Take action quickly, before anxiety has a chance to build and prevent you from making that first step."[9] These values are evident in our child-rearing practices. Today's "helicopter parents" seem determined to micromanage their children's lives to prevent them from experiencing any kind of internal distress. I was talking to an older and wiser colleague about how bad I felt about disappointing my son, and he surprised me by saying "Thank goodness." One of the greatest challenges in parenting is to allow your child to go through the kind of internal tension they need to learn and grow, without interfering to drain the tension and relieve our own anxiety.

SEEKING BALANCE

There is no doubt that letting internal tension build inside of you is an unpleasant experience most people would prefer to avoid. When I go to the gym to work out, the sweating and muscle soreness is uncomfortable and sometimes even painful. There are mornings when I wake up and just do not want to go to the gym, but I get up and work out anyway, because I know that I have to tolerate that short-term discomfort for longer-term gain. In the same sense, hanging in there and tolerating internal tension is unpleasant and can be painful and even disruptive. Resisting the temptation to act out, hanging in there, and tolerating that internal tension is what allows us to make effective and enduring change in our lives.

Psychotherapy and other intimate relationships (see chapter 3) help us hang in there and tolerate our internal tension, and make possible the kinds of core change it is difficult to accomplish on our own. Psychotherapy is simply the process of helping people to hang in there and more fully embrace the full range of their experience (see chapter 7). Therapists, like parents, struggle with our impulses to rescue patients from their own tension. One of the hardest things for new therapists to learn is how to tolerate their patient's tension in the service of change.

Effective change is all about finding the right balance. Research suggests that low to moderate levels of internal tension are more productive than either minimal or high levels.[10] Too much tension can be incapacitating, but too little tension robs us of the essential fuel that drives the process of change. I often use the analogy of stretching to describe seeking this balance. If you have a tight muscle and you want to increase your range of motion, you learn how to stretch that muscle gently. If you do not challenge yourself sufficiently, you will not get the kind of results you are looking for, but if you push too hard you risk tearing the muscle. Similarly, when you are trying to increase your capacity to embrace a fuller range of your experience, you can hang in there to help you tolerate the increasing internal tension. If you push too hard, you risk generating levels of internal tension that are not only ineffective but may cause a significant setback.

PSYCHIATRIC MEDICATIONS

The increasing use of psychiatric medications is an excellent way to talk about seeking the correct balance of internal tension to facilitate change. Initially, psychiatric medications were limited to a variety of sedatives, which were used to sedate patients, but not thought to be specific treatments for any disorder. In the 1950s, a new generation of medications were introduced, creating for the first time pharmacological treatments thought to actually treat particular mental illnesses.[11] More recently, pharmaceutical companies have launched massive advertising campaigns directly to consumers, successfully convincing us to use medications not just to treat illnesses, but also to help relieve us of the normal internal tension generated in daily living, something these medications were never designed for. In recent surveys, eighty-three percent of people believe that psychiatric medications can help them to deal with day-to-day stresses; sixty-eight percent of people believe that medications can help them to feel better about themselves, and seventy-six percent believe that medications can help make things easier in relations with family and friends.[12] This is a significant, and of course, very lucrative, shift in our understating of the purpose of psychiatric medications. The combined sales of antidepressants and antipsychotics jumped from around $500 million in 1986 to nearly $20 billion in 2004, a forty-fold increase.

There is a good deal of psychological research on the efficacy of psychiatric medications versus psychotherapy in the treatment of depression. In most studies, psychiatric medications and psychotherapy combined are more effective than either psychotherapy or medications used alone.[13] The exception was one of the largest studies of depression in which psychotherapy alone outperformed psychotherapy combined with medication, because the outside-in intervention of medication was introduced prematurely, eliciting a backlash in the combined group that decreased its effectiveness.[14]

Using medications alone runs the risk of reducing the level of internal tension too much, and draining the tension necessary to generate change. Using psychotherapy alone runs the risk of stirring up so much internal tension that it interferes with the process of change. Psychiatric medications, like any outside-in intervention, can be used either to help us further embrace our experience or to detach from experience. Medications are most effective when used not to remove internal tension, but to modulate our level of internal tension to a level maximally conducive to the process of change.

6

WHEN TO TRY HARDER AND
WHEN TO STOP TRYING SO HARD

Know what's weird? Day by day, nothing seems to change, but
pretty soon . . . everything's different.

—Calvin, from *Calvin and Hobbes*[1]

You have learned a lot about the process of change in this book. You
have learned that embracing all aspects of your experience is the key
to change, and that you can embrace your experience by either Trying
Harder or Not Trying So Hard. You have learned about being stuck in
the process of change, and how to use intimate relationships to help you
embrace your experience more fully to get unstuck. Now it is time to
put all of the pieces together to create a specific plan for the change you
want to make in your life.

Some parts of our lives are fairly straightforward and uncomplicated,
and either Trying Harder or Not Trying So Hard can be a powerfully
effective way to change. Other areas of our lives are more complex and
multilayered, and relying on either Trying Harder or Not Trying So
Hard alone is not as effective. Months or even years go by and nothing seems to change, and it is hard to understand why it is so difficult
to make this change when we have been so effective in making other
changes in our lives. Change in these more complex areas of our lives

that have resisted simplistic, one-dimensional solutions requires the integration of Trying Harder and Not Trying So Hard approaches. The critical question in the process of change is when to Try Harder or Not Try So Hard. In the process of change, timing is everything.

DOING WHAT YOU LOVE

Laura is forty-three years old, married, and has three children, the youngest of whom started seventh grade this year. Laura grew up in a middle class suburban home. Her father was an engineer and her mother was a homemaker. Laura's dad grew up during the depression and went to work when he was fourteen to help support the family. Laura's father is a very cautious, self-reliant man who taught Laura to get a safe, secure job that she could rely on to support herself.

Laura was a business major in college because her friends thought that was the best path to a successful career. Laura never really liked her business classes, but she figured that suffering through those classes was the kind of short-term sacrifice that grownups make to achieve their long-term goals. Laura's first job out of college was in banking because her father suggested that was a secure career path, and Laura cared more than she wanted to admit about earning her father's all too infrequent approval. Laura was dedicated, worked hard, and gradually advanced to a middle management position in a well-respected bank.

Laura and her husband, Bill, planned to have children. Laura wanted to stay home with the children, but she also thought that her mother made a mistake in not working outside the home. Like most of her peers, Laura wanted to have it all, so she and Bill both worked hard and made the kind of prudent financial decisions that would make it possible for Laura to stay home with the children until they started school.

When she left work after the birth of her first child, Laura was surprised to realize that, outside of missing her coworkers, she felt mostly relieved to be away from work. There was a lot of drudgery and isolation in being a stay-at-home mom, and times when Laura felt like she would kill for some good adult conversation, but when her youngest started first grade Laura didn't feel ready yet to leave her children and go back to work. Laura's desire to stay at home ran against the grain of her fiscal conservatism, and it would put a real crimp in the family's plans for college savings and retirement. Laura and Bill talked it over at length and decided that they could afford for Laura to stay at home until the kids were in middle school.

By the time Laura's youngest child started middle school she had geared herself up to return to work part-time, with an eye toward increasing to full-time in a few years. Like most of us, Laura decided to lead with the approach to change that she was most comfortable and familiar with. Laura used the same Trying Harder strategy that helped her find a job when she first got out of college. She carefully researched dozens of banks, looking for competitive salaries and opportunities for advancement, and just as importantly, Laura checked to see whether each company was family friendly in terms of flexible hours, family leave, and so on.

Unfortunately, Trying Harder did not work as well this time. Laura did find several companies that met her criteria, but for some reason Laura was not very enthusiastic about any of them. Normally a real go-getter, Laura procrastinated about contacting these companies, and when she finally did make the calls very few of the companies were willing to meet with Laura for an informational interview.

Laura decided to hire a career coach to help her generate additional leads and learn how to approach companies more effectively. Laura was still was not very enthusiastic about her job search, but with her coach's help she was able to set up several informational interviews and eventually got an interview for what sounded like the perfect job. A small, rapidly growing bank was looking for someone part-time to develop their loan business and eventually run the department full-time. This was the first company that saw Laura's experience as a mother as an asset rather than a liability, an important part of what Laura might bring to the job.

Laura made it through the first round of interviews and was invited back for a three-hour interview with the president of the bank. The interview was scheduled for 3:00 p.m., which meant that Laura's kids would be home alone for a few hours. Laura was very nervous on the day of the interview, and went through every outfit in her closet before settling on something that she thought looked professional enough. While driving to the interview, Laura started to feel nauseated and noticed tightness in her chest. Laura wrote it off to the burrito she had gulped down at a fast food drive through on the way to the interview and took an antacid, but the discomfort got so much worse that it was difficult for Laura to stay focused during the interview. She was sweating and having difficulty breathing, and it occurred to Laura that she might be having a heart attack.

Somehow Laura managed to make it through the rest of the interview, and then she rushed back home to check on the children. It was only later, as she was making dinner that Laura realized that her symptoms had pretty much disappeared as mysteriously as they first appeared.

Laura made an appointment with her physician who suggested that her symptoms sounded more like a panic attack than indigestion. Her physician prescribed a mild tranquilizer and told Laura to cut back on the stress in her life. Laura was dumbfounded! Going back to work seemed like the first real stress she had taken on in years, and now she was letting her family down just when they needed her most. Laura was determined to buckle down and come through for her family. Unfortunately, the harder Laura pushed herself, the more anxious she got. Interviews were the worst, and things got so bad that Laura started to feel panicked any time she even thought about looking for work. Laura's job search ground slowly and painfully to a halt.

WHERE TO START

On the simplest level, you can choose whether to start Trying Harder or Not Trying So Hard based on what you are trying to change or based on the kind of person you are. If you are trying to change something external, something about how you behave rather than how you feel, then the outside-in strategies of Trying Harder are the logical starting place because it is more likely to produce external change more quickly, change that you and those around you can easily see and recognize. Leading with Trying Harder also makes sense if you need to see results quickly to encourage yourself to keep going, like trying to get in shape. It is also a good place to start if there is some urgency about what you want to change, as when your physician tells you to quit smoking because you have a heart condition or your partner tells you she is going to leave if you if you do not control your drinking. On the other hand, if you are trying to change something internal about your life, something about how you feel rather than how you behave, then it makes more sense to start with the inside-out strategies of Not Trying So Hard. For example, if you are tired of feeling so self-critical or fed up with always feeling down or pessimistic about your life, then Not Trying So Hard is a good place to start.

You can also choose where to start based on the kind of person you are. If you are someone who is well connected to your internal life, in tune with your emotions, attentive and respectful of your body, then the gradual inside-out work of Not Trying So Hard probably has a lot of appeal to you. On the other hand, if you are a very pragmatic person who only believes what you can see, then Trying Harder may be more attractive to you. Right-brained people like artists, therapists, and poets tend to prefer Not Trying So Hard, while left-brained people like engineers, business people, and accountants are more often drawn to Trying Harder.

Trying Harder is also more appealing in the ascendancy of our lives, during our twenties and thirties when we are focused on accomplishing certain external goals: wealth, success, prestige, status, and finding a life partner and starting a family. At some point, the fuel for that ascendancy runs out, like the first stage of a multistage rocket. While that first stage is firing, that's all we think about. It doesn't occur to us that there is any stage but the one we are in, and we just enjoy the power and the thrill of pushing that hard and moving so fast.

Nevertheless, every stage does exhaust itself, no matter how much thrust it has behind it. The outdated stage drops off and falls back to earth, and then we do not have a clue what to do next. We need a second stage, but nothing in the first stage prepares us to anticipate what might

Table 6.1: Where to Start: The Simplest Approach

What You Want to Change	Where to Start
Changing something external or that is urgent	Trying Harder
Changing something internal that is not urgent	Not Trying So Hard
You are a pragmatic person who believes what you can see	Trying Harder
You are an intuitive, feeling person	Not Trying So Hard

come next. In fact, all of the assumptions we live our lives by in the first stage interfere with being able to imagine what the second stage might be like, like the assumption that the fuel of the second stage will burn oxygen as the first stage did. Not Trying So Hard is often the fuel for the second stage of our lives.

Psychological research suggests that eighty percent of the time, it is most effective to begin with the inside-out strategies of Not Trying So Hard, and then shift to the action-oriented strategies of Trying Harder when the timing is right.[2] Yet people lead with a Trying Harder approach to change about ninety percent of the time.[3] The problem with this research, like all research, is that it only tells you what works best for most people in most situations, which may not be a good predictor of what will work best for you in your situation. In reality, when faced with an important change in our lives, most of us will instinctively lead with the approach to change that we are most comfortable and familiar with, regardless of the circumstances. When Laura decided to go back to work, she had every reason to expect that Trying Harder would be the best way for her to find a job. After all, it worked pretty well for her after college, and Laura knew many people who found jobs this same way. Trying Harder is often effective and it feels good to do something.

You can fine-tune your approach to change and be even more effective by matching your initial approach to the intensity of your internal current. Life is like a river with its own current and direction. Each of us also has our own internal current. Your internal current is the strength of unconscious resistance that is stirred up in the process of change. In some areas of our lives, the river is broad and the current gentle. In other places, our constricted capacity for experience narrows the river and increases the intensity of our internal current.

The process of change can be confusing because we tend to underestimate the importance of the current and think it is all about us. The stronger the current, the more that change is about the strength of the current and the less it is about how strong we are or how hard we are willing to swim. This is why we can make such dramatic and enduring change in some areas of our lives, yet the same effort and strategies in other areas can yield little or no results. For example, you may manage to overcome all of the obstacles to leave a loveless but mutually dependent marriage, but cannot seem to go to bed early enough to get enough rest. Or maybe you have learned how to manage the finances of your business with great expertise, but you can't balance your own checkbook or pay your bills on time.

Change is more straightforward when the current is not as strong. In mild to moderate current either Trying Harder or Not Trying So Hard can be an equally effective place to begin. You can set out swimming in just about any direction and manage to get where you want to go; like the person whose doctor tells him he needs to stop smoking, so he quits on the spot after thirty-five years of smoking. In mild to moderate current, if you want to change something external, then leading with the outside-in strategies of Trying Harder makes the most sense because you will see results faster. This is particularly true if there is some urgency to the change you want to make, like trying to lose ten pounds before your high school reunion. On the other hand, if you are trying to change something internal in mild to moderate current, like always feeling responsible for other people, then it makes more sense to lead with the inside-out strategies of Not Trying So Hard.

There are other areas of our lives where the current is stronger. Trying Harder can still be effective in moderate current, but you may have to swim much harder to make any noticeable progress, such as the person who goes back to school four nights a week and endures seven years of hardship to get her degree and land a better-paying job.

When approaching an area that may have stronger current, it is a good idea to pull over and have someone help you scout the rapid from the shore so that you can see where the obstacles are and how to pick your way through, because it is much harder to do that once you are caught

6.2: Where to Start: Gauging the Current

Anticipating mild to moderate current			Anticipating strong current	
Do you need immediate results?			Get help gauging the current.	
Yes	No		Mild to moderate current	Strong current
Try Harder	External Change?	Internal Change?	Need immediate results?	
	Try Harder	Don't Try So Hard	Yes	No
			Try Harder Don't Try So Hard	Don't Try So Hard

up in the current. In retrospect, had Laura talked to her husband, Bill, he might have helped her to recognize that her lack of satisfaction with working in banking in the past and her ambivalence about returning to work both suggested at least moderate current. Even with help, it can be difficult to judge the current while standing on the banks of a river. Sometimes you have to wade in the water to feel the actual strength of the current. It was only as Laura waded into her job search that she realized that the current was stronger than she expected and that Trying Harder alone might not get her where she wanted to go.

In still other places, your internal current may be so strong that you cannot make any progress at all, no matter how hard you try, like the person who has tried every imaginable plan to take better care of herself physically yet falls back into the same unhealthy habits again and again and again. It is usually pretty easy to tell when you are coming up on a place with such strong current. Even if you do not consciously see it coming, the pull of the current will get stronger and stronger the closer you get.

Unlike moderate current where the task is to figure out the best way through, the first question in strong current is whether you should try to run this rapid at all. As the Athenian orator, Demosthenes, said, "He who fights and runs away will live to fight another day."[4] People get in trouble in strong current because they assume that they are going to keep pushing forward no matter what the external or internal conditions are. Some rapids are just too dangerous to run. You might be able to get through them later after the spring runoff, or in a few years when you have more experience, but they are just too dangerous to attempt right now. You have to weigh the risks of continuing with the risks of not going on. For example, let us say you want to lose ten pounds to look good in a bathing suit this summer. You know that trying to lose weight has stirred up an enormous amount of internal current in the past and most of the time you end up gaining twenty pounds after losing ten, so maybe it is too risky to try to lose that weight right now. On the other hand, if you are diabetic and your doctor tells you that you have to lose twenty pounds or you are going to become insulin dependent, then you might have to find a way to tackle this change regardless of how risky it is.

If you decide that the benefits outweigh the risks and you want to attempt to change in the face of strong current, then the wisest course by far is to start by Not Trying So Hard. It is tempting to lead with Trying Harder in strong current when the change you are attempting has some urgency to it, like Jennifer, a patient of mine who had a big term paper due in three days. Jennifer had been through enough crises with term papers to know that there was an almost overwhelming amount of internal current for her around school deadlines. Despite her history, I gave in to the pressure she was feeling, overrode my best instincts, and recommend a series of simple outside-in strategies to Jennifer, like breaking the paper down into smaller pieces, setting deadlines for each piece, and doing something fun to reward herself after finishing each part. Predictably, the strategy was not only ineffective; it precipitated a significant backlash that set Jennifer even further back in her work.

NAVIGATING THE CURRENT

After deciding which approach to start with, the next step in the process of change is learning how to navigate the current. No matter which approach you lead with, somewhere along the way you are bound to run into some resistance because there is some current in almost every part of our lives. Encountering resistance does not necessarily mean that you are on the wrong track and need to change your approach. Rather than seeing resistance as an obstacle, you can use your resistance as a guide to the aspects of your experience that you are having difficulty embracing, in the same way that pain helps physicians diagnose where the problem is. Laura's resistance took the form of her twice putting off returning to work and then uncharacteristically procrastinating once she started to look for a job. Laura's resistance points to her difficulty embracing her ambivalence about leaving her children and returning to work.

For example, if you want to start eating a more healthy diet and your previous attempts have been short-lived, ending with significant self-recriminations, then your resistance is letting you know that you have more current in the area of self-care than you were aware of. Trying to push through that resistance by forcing yourself into another deprivation-based diet is not going to work any better this time than it has in the past. You have to negotiate with your resistance in stronger current or that current will have its way with you. Freud's greatest and most enduring contribution was the unsettling notion that it is our insides, our unconscious, that actually runs our lives. He used the analogy of an iceberg, suggesting that our conscious mind is like the top ten percent of an iceberg that is visible above water. Trying to force change from the outside-in against a strong current is like pushing one way on the top of the iceberg while the current is forcing the bulk of the iceberg in a different direction. Recent research on weight management suggests that you can be more effective by learning how to follow your internal cues than by arbitrarily imposing an outside-in structure like a diet or food plan.[5] In other words, you cannot just banish that craving for a piece of chocolate cake; you have to first make room for the craving, and then negotiate with that urge, as in "Let's make a deal. Would you be satisfied with three bites of that cake?" Alternatively, you might bargain with yourself, "How about if we eat half of the piece of cake and then go for a thirty-minute walk?"

Trying Harder to force change from the outside-in against stronger current is not only ineffective, it can also create a dangerous backlash. Backlash is when we blame ourselves for failing to change something that seems simple and straightforward on the outside, but is actually very psychologically complex and laden with multilayered internal conflicts and ambivalence. Examples are believing that losing weight is simple because all you have to do is eat less and exercise more, or that getting on top of your finances should be straight forward because all you have to do is set aside the time and get it done. Trying to force change from the outside in before we are ready can actually make things worse.[6] For example, in one study people with low self-esteem actually felt worse about themselves after being asked to repeat positive self-aphorisms.[7]

Laura ran into more current than she anticipated in her efforts to return to work. She tried to push herself through her resistance, precipitating a backlash in the form of a panic attack, which was followed by self-critical judgments about letting her family down. Once you are locked into this kind of backlash, Trying Harder will only make things worse. Staying the course just will not work. The only way out of this kind of mess is to make a midcourse correction and Stop Trying So Hard.

MIDCOURSE CORRECTIONS

> A great man always considers the timing before he acts
>
> —Chinese proverb

Whether you start by Trying Harder or by Not Trying So Hard is less important than knowing when to make midcourse corrections. The two most common errors in the process of change are moving prematurely to the outside-in interventions of Trying Harder before you are internally ready, or failing to implement the outside-in strategies of Trying Harder once you are internally ready.[8] In the language of sales, the two most common errors are trying to close the deal before the customer is ready and failing to close the deal when the customer is ready. Timing is everything.

The effective timing of midcourse corrections is all about tracking your sense of internal movement. *Internal movement* is any kind of shift in your internal experience, an increase in your capacity for experience, any sense that something inside of you is changing. For example, you may notice that you are more able to feel compassionate and understanding in situations that used to make you feel irritated and critical, or you may find yourself able to feel angry in situations in which you had formerly been compliant. You may notice that your thinking is more flexible and open in areas in which it was formerly more absolutist and closed to questioning.[9] You may feel more confused and less sure of yourself, more distressed.

In this culture, we tend to rely on external indications of change rather than paying attention to our internal experience. Laura figured her search was going pretty well; she identified several companies that matched her criteria, and was poised on the edge of landing what seemed like the perfect job. Laura's panic attack caught her off guard. It did not occur to Laura that she might need to go through a process of internal discernment, reflecting on what kind of work she would find personally challenging, enjoyable, and satisfying before she could be ready to return to work. In other words, Laura tried to close the sale before she was ready.

Relying on external indicators of change can be misleading because change happens internally long before it is externally visible. The process of change is actually quite complex, even mysterious. Like a solar eclipse, we cannot see the process of change directly. We know it primarily through the shadow it casts, which is the profound impact on our lives. In one experiment, people won or lost money when they picked from a blue or red deck of cards. By measuring the participants' physiological response, researchers were able to determine that the average participant needed only ten trials to internally figure out which deck to pick. However, it took them an average of thirty trials to consciously realize that they had figured it out, and a full fifty trials before they changed externally and began to pick consistently from the blue deck.[10]

You can think of the process of change like a baby chick hatching from its shell. The first visible signs of change are when the chick begins to peck its way through the shell, but there is an ongoing process of internal growth and development leading up to that hatching that is hidden from view. If you could see inside the shell, then you would know if the chick is growing. As long as the chick is developing internally, it does not need any external help to hatch. On the other hand, if the chick is stuck in its internal process, it might need an external intervention, like a baby chick caesarean. If you intervene without first looking inside the shell, you risk interfering with the natural, ongoing process of change.

"Turn Around Norman" is a character in the Tom Robbins novel *Skinny Legs and All*.[11] Norman is a street performer whose act is to stand still. He gathers a crowd around him on the street and does absolutely nothing but stand there. However, if his audience watches him long enough, they can see that he is facing in a different direction than when he started. Even if they watch him every minute, they cannot catch Norman moving a muscle. Nonetheless, slowly, imperceptibly, Norman turns right in front of their eyes and they never see him do it. This is his act: Norman turns a full 360 degrees in front of their eyes while apparently motionless. Once he completes the 360 degrees, he picks up his hat and his money and leaves.[12]

A scientist studied a group of monkeys who ate mostly coconuts. One day, for the first time the scientist observed a monkey taking his coconut to the stream to wash the sand away. The innovation spread slowly throughout the island, until about one hundred monkeys were washing the sand off their coconuts.

What happened next is more difficult to explain. Almost overnight, all of the monkeys on the island began washing the sand off their coconuts. Even more puzzling is that at the same time, all of the monkeys on neighboring islands also began to wash the sand off their coconuts. What makes this difficult to explain is not just how rapidly the change spread, but that the monkeys don't swim, and have no way of traveling or communicating between islands. When we minimize the importance of subtle internal shifts, we are not taking into account the possibility that any small shift may be the hundredth monkey.[13]

It is difficult to make midcourse corrections based on the presence or absence of a subtle and often difficult-to-detect sense of internal movement, sometimes having to overlook compelling evidence that suggests we are either not changing or even moving in the wrong direction. It is easy to misinterpret these indications of internal movement as signs that things are getting worse rather than better, as indicators that you are headed in the wrong direction and need to change course. Following our sense of internal movement is an act of faith in our lived experience. It requires that we find the courage to let go of what we know before having any idea of what might take its place, or even if there will be anything to take its place. Fidelity to internal experience is like standing with one foot on the dock and trying to summon the courage to step onto a boat, only you are blindfolded, don't know where the boat is, and don't have any idea what direction the boat might be headed in. The only thing you can be certain of is that the dock is not going anywhere; it is not going to change. The old saying is "Whenever one door shuts, another one opens," not "Wait until you see what new door will open before you shut the old one."

However, as long as you have a sense of internal movement, then you are in the current of your life and change is underway. When you encounter increased resistance, use either outside-in or inside-out strategies, along with your close relationships to help you embrace the experiences you are having difficulty embracing. If you do not have a sense of internal movement, then there must be aspects of your experience that you are not yet fully embracing. In Laura's case, her lack of enthusiasm for her job search was a good indication of a lack of internal movement, which suggests that there were parts of her experience that Laura had not yet fully embraced.

Regardless of your initial approach, if you do not have senses of internal movement, consider a midcourse correction. If you are Trying Harder and do not have a sense of internal movement, then it is time to Stop Trying So Hard. If you are Not Trying So Hard and don't have any sense of internal movement, then try making judicious use of Trying Harder strategies to help you embrace the experiences you are blocked from experiencing.

Integrating Trying Harder strategies with a Not Trying So Hard approach is like driving a car that is stuck in the snow. You apply the Trying Harder strategies very slowly at first, making sure to go slowly enough to get some traction but not so fast as to spin the wheels. In other words, use Trying Harder strategies to generate enough productive tension to create internal movement but not so much as to generate a backlash. If you have any sense of a backlash as you apply these Trying Harder strategies then back off and resume Not Trying So Hard.

Let's go back now and take another look at Laura's story, using what we have learned to better understand why Laura had such difficulty with what seemed like a straightforward job search, and how we can use the information from this chapter to help Laura succeed in this important life change.

Laura naïvely assumed that she would encounter only mild current in returning to work based on her previous experience, so she did not ask anyone to help her gauge the current. Laura led with Trying Harder because it was what she knew best, and it is the fastest route to observable change.

Laura ran into more current than she expected and her attempts to change did not go very smoothly. Had Laura asked her husband, Bill, for

Table 6.3: When to Try Harder and When to Stop Trying So Hard

Trying Harder		Not Trying So Hard	
Outside-in strategies to embrace experience		Inside-out strategies to embrace experience	
Go with resistance		Go with resistance	
Internal movement?		Internal movement?	
Yes	No	Yes	No
Continue Trying Harder	Stop Trying So Hard	Continue Not Trying So Hard	Judicious use of Trying Harder

help in gauging the current, she could have anticipated at least moderate current and might have chosen a different approach. Laura might still have succeeded by Trying Harder if she had tracked her sense of internal movement rather than relying on external indicators of change, like how many job leads she was generating. Laura thought that she was on the verge of landing a great job when she was invited for a second interview, and her panic attack blind-sided her because she had not been paying attention to the absence of any sense of internal movement.

Laura's panic attack suggested that she was in a backlash, and once she was locked into this kind of backlash, Trying Harder can only makes things worse. Laura's only real option was to Stop Trying So Hard. Laura's impasse lets us know that she was not embracing the full range of her experience. To get unstuck, Laura needed to use her resistance as a guide to help her understand what aspects of her experience she was having difficulty embracing. In this case, Laura's resistance took the form of delaying and then procrastinating about her job search. Laura decided to ask some of her closest friends to help her understand what parts of her experience she was missing that were getting in the way of making this change.

Laura talked to several friends about their jobs. She asked them how they chose their particular careers, how they found their current job, and how much satisfaction they got from their work. Laura was surprised to hear that most of her friends who liked their jobs never had much of a plan; they stumbled into something that seemed enjoyable to them at the time and then followed their hearts from there. Laura understood then what her resistance indicated. Laura's attachment to external goals like earning a certain salary and pleasing her father got in the way of embracing her own internal experience. Laura's job search was unsuccessful because she was not embracing her own interests and excitements.

It was difficult for Laura even to imagine what she might enjoy or find satisfying in a career, so her friend suggested a simple inside-out exercise to help Laura get in touch with her experience. Her friend suggested that Laura make a list of all the things she most liked to do, anything at all, even if it had nothing to do with a possible job, and then pay attention to how she felt about herself when doing each of the things on the list. It was hard for Laura to even come up with a list of things she enjoyed doing, and every time she did come up with something Laura would quickly be tempted to cross it off the list because it wasn't practical. For example, one day while outside working in the garden Laura realized that she really liked working outdoors. Laura enjoyed the sensations of doing hard physical labor, and she felt a real sense of satisfaction and pride at the end of the day when she saw what she had accomplished. Laura started to daydream about what it might be like to do this kind of work for a living, but within a few minutes, she was running figures in her head about the economics of owning a landscaping business and berating herself for even considering such an irresponsible plan.

Laura clearly needed some help allowing herself to embrace the experience of her own interests and excitement, and she cautiously turned to her husband Bill, half expecting him to say aloud the same critical thoughts that she was struggling with herself. To her surprise, Bill listened carefully to what Laura had to say, and, rather than shut her down, Bill actually encouraged Laura to push the envelope further and expand her vision of a possible future.

It was painful for Bill to watch Laura struggle, tripping over her own feet repeatedly, unable to find her way out. Bill suggested that they take a family vacation to a church retreat center that friends had mentioned. Laura initially balked at the idea of dipping into their savings when she was still not working, but Bill convinced her that the trip would be a great chance for the family to be reconnected and that a change of pace that might help Laura get unstuck.

The family had an incredible time together on their vacation, and Laura relaxed in ways she did not even know were possible. The whole family took classes in spiritual practices like prayer and meditation and spent a lot of time outdoors. Everyone helped in the community by doing things like working in the kitchen or the community garden. At first, the kids bickered and complained about being bored, but after a few days, everyone settled into an enjoyable rhythm that was much less tense and felt more intimate than their harried time together at home. Laura met regularly with a spiritual director to help her deepen her own prayer life.

Even with all of this internal work, Laura still did not feel much of a sense of internal movement. The next step was for Laura to carefully integrate selected outside-in strategies to help her generate internal movement. As it turned out, Laura did exactly this without even realizing she was doing it. Laura spent a lot of time working in the community garden. Although she did not plan it this way, working in the garden was an outside-in strategy that helped Laura to embrace the experiences she had been unable to embrace fully.

One day, while working in the garden, Laura realized that she was feeling more energized and alive than she had in a very long time. The sense of internal movement that had been so absent during Laura's ill-fated job search was surging through every part of her body now. Laura realized that it wasn't just working outside in the garden that made her feel this alive, it was the whole package: working in the garden, spending more time with her family, living in community, and attending to her spiritual life. Now that she had done the internal work that she needed to do and felt a strong sense of internal movement, Laura was ready to close the deal.

Laura was initially hesitant to discuss any of this with her family because after years of being the caretaker of everyone else's needs, Laura thought it was selfish to consider asking the family to accommodate her needs. When Laura did take the risk of opening up to her family about what she was experiencing, Laura learned that each member of the family was going through their own process of reevaluating their lives. It turns out Laura was not the only one who was unhappy with the life they had all been living. Even more surprising, the more the family talked, the more it became clear that they were all drawn to similar values: family, community, and a more spiritual life.

Six months later Laura and her family were living in a small Midwestern town where families sit on the porch in the evening and talk to their neighbors passing by. They found a church they are all comfortable with, and Laura has been meeting regularly with the minister to talk about her life. Laura and Bill started their own landscaping business and the kids help after school and on weekends.

PUTTING IT ALL TOGETHER

Now let us apply what you have learned in this chapter in looking at three different people all trying to change their adult relationships with their families. In the following examples, Kathy anticipates only mild current in making this change, Nancy expects at least moderate current, and Paul is fairly certain he is going to run into strong current in making this change. Walking through these steps should help you formulate the most effective plan for the change you are contemplating in your life.

Change in Mild Current

Kathy is a young woman in her early 30s who has lived on her own for over a decade. Kathy anticipates only mild current in her ongoing efforts to change her relationship with her family. She has only minimal internal conflicts and ambivalence about taking on more of an adult role in her family, her parents support her growing independence, and Kathy's process of individuation has gone pretty well so far. In mild current, Kathy can be successful leading with either Trying Harder or Not Trying So Hard. Kathy's goals are both external and internal; she wants to change both the way she behaves and the way she feels with her family. Kathy decided to lead by Trying Harder because it is the fastest path to making observable changes in her relationship with her family and there is minimal risk of making things worse.

Kathy chose outside-in strategies to help her to embrace rather than detach from all of her experience, not just the times when she does feel more adult with her family, but also experiences like the delicious regressive pull to be cared for by her parents. Kathy reflected on the roles and rituals that conveyed adult status in her family, such as paying for dinner when the family eats out, talking about her hopes and accomplishments at work, or making independent choices about whether to join in with certain family activities. Taking on some of these new external roles helped Kathy to embrace more fully her experience of herself as an adult in the family.

It is always helpful to recruit a support system to help you embrace the experiences you need to change. The more powerful the current, the more helpful it is to have an ally. Kathy's boyfriend, Matt, came home with her, and Kathy asked Matt to help her anticipate the kinds of situations that typically hook her into a more regressed place, and then plan some strategies together for how to stay more fully herself in those situations. Kathy and Matt agreed that he would signal her whenever he saw her slipping into that one-down place with her family. They also planned some private time together each day to reconnect with each other and help Kathy get firmly grounded in her own experience.

Things rarely go as smoothly as planned, and Kathy did run into some internal resistance in trying to make this change. Kathy noticed that she did sometimes put herself down in subtle ways, or go along with family plans when she really did not want to. Rather than trying to push through her resistance, Kathy used her resistance as a guide to help her understand that, although she was doing a pretty good job overall at being more authentic with her family, financial matters were much harder. Understanding this, Kathy focused her efforts on embracing the financial aspects of being an adult member of her family; she talked with her parents about her recent promotion and salary increase, and insisted on paying the check the next time the family went out to dinner.

Kathy could feel the kinds of internal shifts that let her know that her role in the family was changing over the course of her visit home. Kathy did a good job at staying focused on her own sense of internal movement, and not getting caught up in whether her family was treating her differently, or even if she was acting differently yet. As long as Kathy continues to have that sense of internal movement, then change is underway and she is on the right track.

On the other hand, if Trying Harder did not generate any sense of internal movement, then Kathy would need to consider a midcourse correction and Stop Trying So Hard. If Kathy had any indication of a backlash, such as slipping more often into younger roles, feeling bad about herself, or making self-critical judgments about herself, then it would be even more important for her to Stop Trying So Hard.

Change in Moderate Current

Nancy is a woman in her 40s who has also been trying to change her relationship with her family for quite some time, but she is anticipating at least a moderate amount of current. Nancy's parents are not very open to seeing their daughter in more of an adult role. In fact, sometimes it seems to Nancy like the harder she tries, the more her parents resist. Nancy has tried just about everything that she can think of, yet somehow she always seems to end up feeling sucked right back into the same old ways of being with her family that Nancy has done since she was very little.

Because Nancy anticipated at least a moderate current during her visit home, she decided to ask her sister, Beth, for some help in planning the trip. Nancy knows that once she gets home she will be too caught up in the current to have much perspective. Beth knows the territory well, but is not quite as caught up in the current as Nancy is. Nancy asked Beth to help her review her last few visits home, to help her gauge the potential strength of the current during this visit, and to help Nancy figure out where the obstacles might be and what the best way through is.

The stakes are higher for Nancy than they were for Kathy because in moderate current there is a greater chance of precipitating a backlash and making things worse. Whereas Kathy changed her relationship with her family from the outside in, Nancy decided to approach the same change from the inside out. Kathy started with clear goals and objectives, but Nancy's task is to let go of her family's expectation of what an adult is, and let go of her own expectations of what an adult is and just allow herself to be all of who she authentically is while being with her family.

In talking with her therapist, Nancy realized that she has the same struggle with being fully herself in most of the close relationships in her life, not just with her family. Nancy's therapist suggested that group therapy was the most powerful way to work on this issue because group provides a symbolic family that stirs the emotional pot and helps members to reexperience some of their relational patterns rather than just talking about them.

Not Trying So Hard was particularly difficult for Nancy because she has already been trying to change her relationship with her family for years. Nancy's therapist reminded her to stay focused on her sense of internal movement during this visit and not get distracted by whether she acted more like an adult when she was with her family, but to stay focused on whether there were internal shifts in how she felt. In fact, although Nancy joined the therapy group several months before her visit home, only the most observant family members noticed any change. Internally, however, Nancy felt less anxious, more self-confident, and more like herself than she had ever imagined being with her family. As long as Nancy feels that kind of internal movement, then she should continue Not Trying So Hard, even if her behavior has not changed one little bit. On the other hand, if Nancy did not feel any sense of internal movement through Not Trying So Hard, she should consider the judicious use of the same kind of Trying Harder strategies that Kathy used.

Change in Strong Current

Paul is a man in his 50s who has been distant from his family for many years, so he is pretty sure he is going to run into significant current during this visit home. It took years for Paul to acknowledge himself as a gay man, and it is only recently that Paul has been able to talk about it to even his closest friends. Paul's parents have also made enough comments about homosexuality over the years for Paul to know that he is not walking into a receptive environment.

This is an easy call for Paul because he is fairly certain there is strong current ahead. In sailing, we say, "If you are wondering whether it's time to reef the sails [reduce the amount of sail to prepare for stronger winds], then it's past time." The answer is in the question. If you find yourself asking whether there is strong current ahead, then assume that there is and proceed by Not Trying So Hard.

Leading with Not Trying So Hard means that Paul has to let go of his agenda of trying to change his family and focus instead on coming to terms with his own internal issues about his sexuality before trying to incorporate that change into his relationships with his family. Joining a support group for gay men helped Paul to see his resistance more clearly, and let him know where he was still stuck in the process of fully embracing his experience of himself as a gay man. For example, Paul's group helped him see that keeping this secret gave him a certain protective distance from his family and the thought of being out with his family made Paul feel uncomfortably vulnerable.

Over the years, Paul got used to keeping this secret from his family, but now that he has started to come out in the rest of his life, it is much more difficult to remain hidden with his family. Paul's group wisely counseled patience, and advised him not to focus on whether other people would accept him but to continue to do the internal work on accepting himself. Other members let Paul know that this process could take years, but that as long as Paul has a sense of internal movement, as long as he continues to experience shifts in his acceptance of himself as a gay man, then he should continue Not Trying So Hard.

On the other hand, if Paul does not have any sense of internal movement in his process of self-acceptance after an extended period of Not Trying So Hard, then he can consider the judicious use of outside-in strategies to help him embrace what he is blocked from experiencing. Paul needs to be very cautious because there is such a high risk of creating a backlash when navigating in current of this strength. Paul needs to take it very easy when adding outside-in interventions, giving it just enough gas to get some traction but not so much to make the wheels spin. For example, listing his boyfriend's name in the church phone directory was an outside-in step that Paul was ready to take, but the mere thought of coming out at work made his wheels spin. Of course, if there is any indication of backlash, Paul needs to back off his outside-in interventions and patiently resume Not Trying So Hard.

CONCLUSIONS

Here is a summary of the steps to take to more fully embrace your experience and change your life.

- Decide what you want to change about your life. Is it something external about your behavior or the circumstances of your life, or something about your internal experience?
- Decide whether you want to start the process of change from the outside in by Trying Harder or from the inside out by Not Trying So Hard.
- Begin paying closer attention to what you want to change to learn which aspects of your experience you are not fully embracing.
- Make room for all of your experience, particularly the parts of your experience you are avoiding or having difficulty embracing.
- Take responsibility for your experience rather than blaming others for the circumstances of your life.
- Let yourself know what you know.
- Use your relationships to help you further embrace the aspects of your experience you are having difficulty embracing.
- Look for any places you are stuck, places you are separated from your experience.

- Hang in there and tolerate productive tension.
- Make any midcourse corrections based on tracking your sense of internal movement. As long as you have a sense of internal movement, stay with the same approach. If you do not have a sense of internal movement, consider switching approaches to help you embrace aspects of your experience more fully.

EXERCISE

In conclusion, please take out your notes from the exercise you did in the Preface. Review what you wrote about your experience of change and compare it with what you have learned in this book. How does this model of change compare with your own experience? Is this a model that will help you create the change you want to see in your life? Feel free to embrace whatever you have learned here that makes sense to you in light of your own experience, and leave behind whatever does not fit. There also may be parts you want to chew a bit more to see if that makes them easier to digest, and other parts you may want to put in a to-go container to look at another time.

7

TENDING THE GARDEN: HELPING OTHERS CHANGE

You must be the change you wish to see in the world.

—Gandhi[1]

May I see in all those who suffer, only the fellow human being.

—Maimonides

EXERCISE

In the introduction, I invited you to reflect on your own experience of change, and use those reflections to guide you in your reading of this book. I would like to suggest a similar exercise as you begin this chapter. Please take a moment and reflect on some of the relationships in your life that have most helped you change and grow as a person, to become more fully yourself. This may be your relationship with your parents, your life partner, a friend, therapist, and clergy: whoever has been helpful to you in the important changes in your life. Please list some of the characteristics of those relationships that were most helpful, as well as characteristics of those relationships that were less helpful, and may have even interfered with the change you wanted to make. When you finish this chapter, please go back and review this list in light of what you learn in the chapter.

This chapter is for parents, teachers, lovers, therapists, clergy, and anyone else interested in helping someone change. (There is a section at the end of the chapter written specifically for psychotherapists.) The central premise of this book is that change happens through the process of embracing experience, so the best way to facilitate change in others is to help them embrace their experience more fully. Relationships are one of the most powerful vehicles to help us embrace aspects of our experience that we have difficulty accessing (see chapter 3). The question in this chapter is, how can we best be in relationship with others to help them change by embracing the full range of their experience?

HELPING OTHERS CHANGE VERSUS TRYING TO CHANGE OTHERS

> What is the difference between a man and a light bulb? You can change a light bulb.
>
> —Anonymous

Richard was an agricultural expert who worked for the Peace Corps in a country in which many people starved every year. The country had rich volcanic soil, but the people had not yet learned to rotate their crops so the soil was depleted, and they did not have any chemical pesticides or fertilizers so their crops were ravaged by disease. Richard brought fertilizers and pesticides, and taught the people how to rotate their crops, and soon the village was producing more than enough to feed everyone. After a couple of years, Richard's time of service was over, so he returned home.

Some years later, a friend told Richard that he had been to the village where Richard had worked, and they had run out of pesticides and fertilizer, stopped rotating their crops, and the people were once again starving. Richard returned to the village, this time on his own and not as a part of any government program. Richard did something he had not done on his first trip. Richard approached the village elders and asked them if he might have a piece of land to farm. The elders were puzzled, because they did not think of land as something that could be owned, so they told Richard he was welcome to farm any empty piece of land.

Richard lived on this piece of land; he rotated his crops, used organic pesticides and fertilizers, and soon grew more than enough food to share with his neighbors. This time Richard did not try to teach anyone anything. After several years, the village elders approached Richard and asked him to show them how he grew so much food.

In another example, my son was an avid soccer player. He played with passion and abandon. At thirteen, he experienced his first injury serious enough to keep him from playing for a while. He was chomping at the bit to get back, but when he returned to playing, he was uncharacteristically cautious and timid. He seemed to have lost the confidence and aggression that are necessary to be successful at a competitive level.

This went on for almost a year. I talked to him after every game about what I saw. I told him that he was not going after players on defense, not making hard challenges on 50-50 balls, and that he seemed reluctant to tackle when he needed to. I shared my own experience as an athlete with him. I told him that while I certainly understood his instinct to protect himself, that all of my serious injuries had come while playing less than full out. I did everything I could think of, but nothing helped. I do not know what that year was like for him, but it was agonizing for me. I approached each game with dread because it was so painful to watch him struggle, to see him playing so far below the level of his ability, and to sit there week after week helpless to do anything about it.

On the morning of a tournament he woke up and told his mother, "I think I have been playing too cautiously because of my injury," as if he had never heard those words before in his life, which in some ways he had not. My wife, in her great wisdom, said little in reply. That weekend he played all out, fearlessly, better than ever before. Apparently, once he "got it," change was the easiest thing in the world. I have no idea if my repeated talking to my son interfered or helped in some way with his "getting it." No doubt, like Toad, I spent all those months talking to my son mainly to have something to ease my own sense of helplessness. I just know that he had to "get it," before he could change.

Effective and enduring change is best facilitated when we strive to help others change rather than trying to change others. Change is a naturally occurring process that happens with or without professional help because the process of change in professional settings is simply a distilled version of the same naturally occurring process of change.[2] As a result, the majority of people make significant life changes without professional help. Fewer than five percent of smokers, ten percent of alcoholics or obese people, and twenty-five percent of people with mental health disorders ever seek professional help.

When you undertake to help someone else change, it is helpful to think of your role as more of a catalyst than a cause of change. Jerome Frank compared the role of a psychotherapist to that of a midwife, saying, "What he [sic] does may make a lot of difference in how smoothly or rapidly the process occurs, but the extent to which he causes it is uncertain."[3] Similarly, the great Renaissance artist Michelangelo said he created sculptures by removing whatever did not belong, whatever was interfering with the full expression of what was latent within the stone. Michelangelo said of his famous sculpture "David," "There is an angel inside of the rock and I am setting him free."[4] When we attempt to help others change, our job is to help them get past whatever impasse is preventing them from embracing the full range of their experience, to help them set free the angel hidden within.

It is easy to get caught up in trying to change other people without even realizing you are doing it. We have our own agendas for other people, often without being aware of them. We want other people to change either because we think it would be better for us, or because we believe we know what is best for them, a kind of psychological imperialism. It is important to think through the ways in which our agendas, overt and covert, may be influencing the process of change for others.

You might think helping others change rather than trying to change them is as straightforward as asking the other person what he or she wants. The nature of relationships, however, makes it difficult to be clear about what we want apart from our desire to meet the expectations of others, also known as codependency. Do I really want Chinese food right now, or am I just going along with what everyone else in the family wants? Just because someone does not object to our suggestions for change does not mean they have fully signed on. We should aspire to the standard of informed consent in any effort to help someone else change. *Informed consent* is a legal term used in research studies to make sure that participants not only understand what they have signed up for, but are also under no form of coercion to participate, like the subjects in a professor's class who are worried about not getting a good grade if they don't sign up for his study.

When we undertake to help someone else change, it is important to be curious, and at times even suspicious, about our own covert agendas. For example, if I propose that my wife and I start a diet together in the New Year, am I trying to get her to support me in losing weight or surreptitiously trying to trick her into losing weight? When I sign my six-year-old son up for soccer and buy him all the fanciest equipment, how much am I supporting his interest and how much am I trying to relive my own thwarted athletic dreams, especially if I have not even asked him yet if he wants to play soccer?

I find this issue very salient in my work with couples, particularly heterosexual couples in which gender role stereotypes make it difficult for women to find their full voice. Men often act unilaterally on their agenda for the couple, believing they have heard their partners and know what is best. There is a comically extreme example of this dynamic in the movie *Feast of Love*.[5] A man decides unilaterally to help his wife get over her fear of dogs by buying her a puppy for her birthday. Outraged by his complete misunderstanding of what she needs and his arrogant disregard of her feelings, she actually leaves him.

Even when you are clearly supporting someone else's freely chosen agenda for change, it is important to monitor your own level of investment in that person's agenda. Things never go well when you are more invested in other people's change than they are. Your over-investment makes you a convenient target for them to externalize their resistance and fight with you rather than embrace their own internal tension. Anyone who has been around adolescents is painfully familiar with this dynamic, because young adults are notorious for picking fights with others to avoid dealing with their own internal tension. The more invested you get in an adolescent changing in a particular way, the more they dig in their heels and resist, even if it's what they actually want for themselves. Parents can be so caught up in making sure that their adolescent children are on the "right path" that they lose sight of the fact that it is their job to help their children choose their own paths.

Trying to change others is not only disrespectful; it is also ineffective, because our resistance to being changed is stronger than our resistance to changing ourselves. The single most important thing I learned in graduate school, what I think of as my mantra for psychotherapy, is, "Any patient can defeat any therapist at any time" (R. Felder, personal communication, 1984). This mantra applies to any relationship in which you are trying to help someone else change. Any employee can defeat any employer at any time, any student can defeat any teacher at any time, any child can defeat any parent at any time, and of course, any reader can defeat any author at any time.

THE HELPING RELATIONSHIP

As we discussed in chapter 1, there is a strong preference in our culture for outside-in approaches to change. We much prefer to *do* something, and not just sit there. As you might expect, this same bias is evident in our approaches to helping people change. We believe the best way to help people is to give them advice, to tell them what they should do to reduce the level of internal tension they (and perhaps we) are feeling.

We have a less well-developed understanding of helping people change from the inside out by helping them tolerate their internal tension. We tend to underestimate the power of having someone sit with you and simply encourage you to embrace your experience. Here is a story of a relationship in which someone's unexpected willingness to just be with another's experience without trying to change him was a very powerful force for change.

A family took their young child to a fancy restaurant for dinner, the kind of restaurant with linen napkins and nice glasses that make parents with young children nervous. The server approached the table and took first the mother's and then the father's order. The server then asked the young child what he would like to eat, and the little boy blurted out "I want a hot dog with French fries and a Coke!" The mother very calmly interjected, saying, "He will have the baked chicken, mashed potatoes, and green beans with a glass of milk." The server never broke eye contact with the little boy, and the ensuing silence made everyone a little uncomfortable. The server then asked the little boy, "Ketchup or mustard?" Now there really was an awkward silence at the table. This was new territory for everyone in the family, and no one knew quite what to do. Finally, hesitantly the young boy replied "Ketchup, please." The server took his order and walked away. The young boy turned to his mother and said, "Mommy, that lady thinks I'm real!" (R. Felder, personal communication, 1985).

Listening

> True Listening is worship.
>
> —Heidegger[6]

In chapter 2, we talked about putting experience into words as a powerful tool for embracing experience. For every act of talking, there must be a complementary act of listening, the hearing that gives meaning to the tree falling in the forest. The experience of talking to someone is quite different from talking to oneself. In fact, in our culture talking to oneself is regarded with some suspicion. Throughout history, there have been culturally sanctioned healers to talk to, whether a shaman, clergy person, or psychotherapist. Listening is one of the most powerful, yet often overlooked ways to help others further embrace their experience.

On the face of it, listening seems so simple, something we do reflexively, without much conscious thought. At the same time, we are aware of subtleties in listening, because we think of some people as "good listeners" or "easy to talk to." In trying to help others change, we are particularly interested in the kind of listening that facilitates what we called *productive talking* in chapter 2, the kind of talking that helps people to embrace rather than separate from their experience.

Everyone listens in his or her own unique way. Many people listen primarily to the words someone speaks, but other people listen more to emotional tone than words, and others tune more into body language or other intangibles. My teacher was a concert pianist who kept a piano in his office. He would frequently invite patients to play a duet with him in session. Whether they played piano was irrelevant, he just wanted to listen to the music they created together. I grew up in a verbal, intellectual family in which the precision of the spoken word was highly valued. Not surprisingly, as therapist, I listen carefully to the words that patients use, intentionally or unintentionally, and the deeper meanings those words may convey. I pay careful attention to the initial, seemingly casual exchange in a session, even if it is while walking down the hall to my office. A patient recently asked me how it was to be back from vacation, and said it was always a difficult adjustment for him to "return to the inertia." We spent the entire session talking about his ambivalence and conflict about his work, and his struggles to discern vocation from avocation.

It does not really matter what particular expression of a person's experience you focus on as a listener. They are all reflections of that person's experience, so they all lead to the same source. The various expressions of our experience are like the threads of a tapestry. It does not matter which thread you start with because they are all interconnected, and whichever thread you follow will eventually connect you with all the others.

In this section we will talk about three types of listening that facilitate change: listening to the manifest content of the speaker, listening to the latent content of the speaker, and listening relationally to your own experience as well as the speaker's.

Listening to Manifest Content

Listening to the manifest content is the most basic kind of listening: the type of listening that is most familiar to us. This is a literal hearing, not a hearing between the lines or a hearing that extends beyond what is spoken, but hearing the speaker's meaning as it is overtly given.

Listening to the manifest content requires the capacity to set aside your own experience in order to hear the speaker's experience as it is given, rather than hearing what we expect to hear or what we want to hear. This is a "good listener," someone who sets aside his or her own experience in order to listen fully to what you are saying. This is the kind of listening that therapists often teach couples when they believe that communication problems are at the heart of marital difficulties. These therapists teach their patients to "mirror" their partner, first repeating, "What I hear you saying is . . . " and then checking that for accuracy before moving on to what the partner wants to say in response.[7]

While this seems straightforward, it is actually more challenging than you might think. It is difficult to listen to someone else's experience as they actually lived it without automatically translating that experience into our own frame of reference. For example, when we listen to a friend talk about problems in his marriage, it is difficult to not translate his experience into our own frame of reference, and think about his marital problems in relationship to our own marriage. Then we step in to offer advice based on what has been helpful to us, but that advice comes more from attending to our own experience than any real hearing of our friend's difficulties.

In an all too common example, a wife starts talking to her husband about something that is bothering her. Listening from his own frame of reference, the husband hears his wife bringing him a problem that she wants his help solving, so he starts offering suggestions. From the wife's frame of reference, she is talking to her husband about something that is troubling her and just wants him to hear her. Every time he offers a solution, she feels unheard. The husband is incredulous when his wife tells him he is not listening, because not only is he listening carefully to his wife, but he is Trying Harder to be helpful as well.[8]

Listening to Latent Content

While we value a good listener and we work hard at getting it right when listening to others, imagine how frustrating it would be to talk with someone who just repeated everything you said to him or her. Every couple has had this fight: one partner complains that the other is "not listening" and the other partner "proves" he or she has been listening by repeating back everything the first partner just said. He or she listened to the words spoken, and does not understand why the first partner still does not feel heard. Feeling truly heard in a conversation comes from the second type of listening, which includes listening to the latent as well as the manifest content of the speaker, hearing "between the lines." Research suggests that only about twenty percent of what we understand from others comes from what they say,[9] so when we just listen to the manifest content, we are missing about eighty percent of what someone is trying to communicate.

We credit Freud with the idea that all communication has a symbolic unconscious meaning underlying the manifest conscious meaning. When we listen to just the manifest content of another's words, they are likely to stay stuck at the conscious manifest level of what the person is talking about. When we listen for the latent content of another's words, we can help that person more fully embrace the aspects of experience that are latent in those words. In other words, I become more fully myself when someone listens fully to the latent content of what I am saying.

Just as was true of listening to manifest content, truly hearing the latent content of what someone is saying requires a radical fidelity to the other's experience as he or she lived it with as few presuppositions as possible. It is only when we are able to bracket our own expectations of another's experience that we can facilitate the emergence of the latent aspects of another's experience.

For example, imagine a friend is talking to you about a new job she is applying for. The manifest content of what she is saying is about her feeling insecure about whether she can get the job, or if she is qualified for the job, or being scared to let herself get too excited and risk feeling disappointed. You hear the manifest content of what your friend is saying, but you also notice a sense of excitement about her: her eyes are wide open; she is speaking rapidly and leaning forward, and, despite how hard she is trying to convince herself, she does sound excited. You may share this observation with your friend, "You know it's funny, you are talking about being scared and unsure of yourself, but I keep getting the sense that you are excited too." Alternatively, you may say nothing at all about your awareness of the latent meaning of what she is talking about. In either case, whether you say anything to your friend, just being aware of the excitement latent in her speaking will help your friend more fully embrace that aspect of her experience that she has been largely unaware of.

Listening Relationally

The third type of listening is attending to your own experience while also listening to someone else speaking. This type of listening happens primarily in intimate relationships, and we will take it up in more depth in the section for psychotherapists at the end of the chapter.

It is counterintuitive to suggest that listening to your own experience enhances your ability to hear someone else. It seems that your job as a listener is to block out as much of your own experience as you can in order to focus on hearing someone else's experience. That makes sense from an intrapsychic perspective, but if we look at the process of listening from a relational perspective (see chapter 3), we understand that speaking never happens in a vacuum. We do not speak to ourselves; we speak to others, even if they are not physically present. Pause for a moment and consider something important that is going on in your life that you might like to speak to someone about. Now think about three or four people you might like to talk with about this, and imagine talking with each one of those people. Notice that you speak differently in each imagined conversation, because the relationship you have with each person helps you embrace different aspects of the experience.

Your experience of speaking in each of those imagined situations is different because the experiences of speaking and listening are both relational experiences. Your experience as a speaker is co-constituted by the experience of the listener, meaning that you cannot fully understand your own experience as a speaker without also understanding something about the experience of the listener.

Let us go back to the example from the previous section of a friend talking to you about a job she has applied for. This time imagine that you have been unemployed for six months. As you listen to your friend, your own experience keeps pushing into your awareness. You are scared you will not find a job, you are worried about losing your home, and the financial stress is affecting your marriage and your relationship with your kids. You are jealous of your friend and angry with her for talking about her good news without considering how it will affect you.

If you don't say anything to your friend about your experience as a listener, your friend will still sense that something is going on with you, and in the absence of any information from you she will draw her own conclusions with the information she has available, which is her own experience. She may conclude that you do not care about her, that you think this is the wrong job for her, or that she is not being a good friend to you. It certainly is not likely that your friend will get in touch with her latent excitement about the potential job. If, however, you share with your friend something of what is going on with you, the two of you may be able to talk through what is going on in the relationship in a way that helps you embrace your caring and excitement for your friend and helps her do the same.

EXERCISE

Please go back and review now what you wrote in the exercise at the beginning of this chapter. How does what you learned in this chapter fit with your experience in helping relationships? Feel free to embrace whatever you have learned here that makes sense to you in light of your own experience. Please feel equally free to discard anything that you read that does not fit with your own experience. Again, there may be parts that do not fit for you now that you may want to come back to another time.

FOR THERAPISTS

This final section of this chapter is designed specifically for psychotherapists and anyone whose professional focus is on helping others change. I was hesitant about including a section for therapists because I do not want to suggest that there are any arcane, secret approaches to change that are appropriate only for therapists. Quite the contrary: research demonstrates that the process of change in psychotherapy is simply a distilled version of the process of change in everyday life.[10,11] At the same time, there are issues of interest to therapists and other professionals that may not be of interest to the average reader.

Embracing Experience: A Radical Fidelity to Lived Experience

Perhaps the most important characteristic that the therapist brings to the helping relationship is a radical, immutable fidelity to the patient's experience as he or she lives it. This means eschewing diagnoses, treatment plans, or anything else that calls us to stand outside of our lived experience and make judgments. Therapists sometimes confuse the role of an attorney with that of a judge. If we believe that reality is defined in objective, consensual terms, then the therapist's job is to judge, to challenge the patient's world view, correcting the patient's "reality testing" by asserting our objective reality over the patient's subjective experience and bringing his or her perception more in line with consensual reality. If we believe that reality is inherently subjective, then the therapist is more like an attorney, trying to hear what the patient has to say in a way that will invite him to embrace his experience more fully.

For example, a patient may report experiences of being hurt in romantic relationships, and conclude that he is deficient in the skills required to love and be loved. It is easy to imagine myself disagreeing with this patient's conclusions, and trying to cleverly find instances that contradict this assumption about himself. I may point to examples of people in his life who do love him, or point out that he seems to do fine in some contexts and struggle in others. In effect, I would be trying to argue him out of his own reality. This approach seems reasonable enough, but the problem is that I am probably just the most recent in a long line of caring people who have attempted this very same strategy. The fact that this person has found his way to my office suggests that talking him out of his reality has not been a very effective strategy.

Rather than challenging the validity of the patient's reality, I could instead point out that his assumptions about not knowing how to love and be loved are judgments; they are derivatives of experience, not lived experience, so they are stagnant rather than dynamic. I could then try to help this patient to articulate and embrace whatever lived experience precedes those judgments.

A dear friend tells the story about a time when her oldest child was three years old and could not get to sleep because he believed there was a crocodile under his bed that was going to hurt him. My friend tried repeatedly to convince him that he was mistaken, that there was no crocodile in the room. All to no avail. Finally, in a flash of creative insight inspired by desperation, she left the room and returned with an imaginary shotgun. After giving the crocodile three chances to leave peacefully, she shot the crocodile, slung it over her back, and hauled the carcass out of the room. Her son fell right asleep, smiling contentedly (A. Greene, personal communication, 1991).

As a field, psychotherapy has a long and conflicted relationship with the matter of the patient's experience. In its infancy, psychology adopted the reductionism of the physical sciences, limiting its data to what can be observed and quantified. Paradoxically, this eliminated the subject of consciousness from the science of the study of consciousness. The definition of the field of psychology (from the Greek *psyche,* meaning "consciousness," and *logos,* meaning "study") in introductory textbooks changed over time from the science of the study of human consciousness to the science of the study of human behavior because behavior is the only aspect of human experience that can be operationalized.

This brings to mind an old story my father used to tell about a cop who comes across an obviously inebriated man late at night on his hands and knees, apparently searching for something under a street light. The cop asks, "Hey buddy, what are you looking for?" and the man replies that he has lost his car keys. The cops asks if he lost them under the street light, and the drunk replies, "No, but the light is a lot better here." There is no question that reducing the complexity of lived experience to what can be seen under the light of the scientific method allows us to bring powerful statistical analyses to bear, but what if the keys are not under the light?

Freud originally trained as a neurologist, and in his early work, he sought to describe the human mind solely in quantitative, physiological terms.[12] However, Freud was profoundly impacted by his training with Jean-Martin Charcot on the treatment of hysteria. Freud came to agree with Charcot that hysteria was caused by childhood sexual trauma.[13] They discovered that the symptoms of hysteria were alleviated by a radical fidelity to their patient's lived experience, by creating a setting that encouraged their patients to talk about their repressed experiences, what Freud later came to call "the talking cure." What was remarkable about these developments was the collaborative nature of the relationship between doctors and patients, and the extent to which their male doctors validated the self-reported experience of female patients. "For a brief decade men of science listened to women with a devotion and a respect unparalleled before or since."[14]

Shortly thereafter, however, Freud repudiated his traumatic theory of the origins of hysteria for a variety of personal and sociopolitical reasons.[15] Freud abandoned his radical fidelity to his patient's experience, and his clinical work changed accordingly. He moved away from the "talking cure" in which the therapeutic effect is located in the actual act of the patient's talking about his or her lived experience witnessed by a therapist who validates and embraces that experience, to a focus on interpretation as the therapeutic effect. The patient's own lived experience is no longer privileged, but is understood instead as a distorted version of the external unseen reality that the analyst is best suited to interpret.[16]

Herman points to Freud's last case study of hysteria, the case of Dora, as the turning point.[17] In this case, the therapeutic relationship was transformed from a mutually respectful collaboration to a relationship that has been described as "emotional combat."[18] While Freud does validate Dora's report of sexual abuse by her father, he analyzes away her feelings of outrage and humiliation, interpreting them as a reflection of her hidden feelings of sexual excitement. In a remarkably healthy act of resistance, Dora terminated her treatment, which Freud interpreted as hostile and vengeful.

Helping Others Change versus Trying to Change Others

> I don't do anything. I can't do anything other than wait with a certain trust in God, until a conflict, endured with patience and braveness, allows for a resolution, which I could not foresee, but which was destined to this person.
>
> —Carl G. Jung

This is a tough one for therapists. The curricula of training programs in all of the mental health disciplines emphasize courses in psychopathology, diagnosis, assessment, theories of personality, and formulating treatment plans. All of these courses are a part of training therapists to believe that we know best what is wrong with other people and what they need to do to change. Patients tell us what is troubling them, which we euphemistically refer to as the "presenting problem," meaning this is what the patient thinks is what is wrong with him, but we understand the underlying issue that is really causing the problem. In my practice, I always fill out any external requests for information collaboratively with the patient in session because I believe that my patients are the authority on their own experience, and because my parents taught me that it is rude to talk about people behind their back.

It is true that there are aspects of our experience that we are unaware of, and that others maybe have a better perspective on. A simple example is my own rear end, which I see infrequently and then only with a distorted view, while those behind me have an unimpeded perspective. However, when we give others privileged perspective on our own experience, we risk pathologizing ourselves. Therapists generally encourage patients to trust their own experience rather than seeing themselves through the eyes of others. The exception seems to be the therapeutic relationship in which we may unknowingly teach people to distrust their own experience.

When patients disagree with us about what is wrong with them or how they should change, we call that resistance, again based on the assumption that we know more about patients than they do themselves. Freud believed that resistance was one of the primary impediments to progress in psychotherapy. Alfred Adler, on the other hand, suggested that resistance is the patient's very healthy inclination to disagree with his therapist or anyone else telling them what to do.[19]

I sometimes hear therapists discussing a patient's psychotherapy in very linear terms such as "We are working on his rage now, but eventually we will have to get to the pain that is underneath that rage." I vacillate between judging myself as stupid because I do not have that same kind of foresight about my patients' therapy and feeling irritation at the therapist's belief that she knows more about what the patient needs than the patient does. It is arrogant for the therapist to decide that no change is taking place in the psychotherapy, or that change is not taking place fast enough. The therapist's impulse to "do something" is a reflection of her struggle to contain the tension generated by the patient's experience. This understanding obviously stands in conflict with a managed care system that holds the therapist responsible for the progress of the psychotherapy.

In addition to our professional training, there are also strong social roles and expectations that reinforce people to look to psychotherapists for answers. Pop psychology and media shrinks have taken the place of clergy as the place to turn to for guidance in our lives. People come to therapy in distress, having exhausted everything they can think of to feel better, and they come to us looking for answers. The culture and the psychotherapist persuade the patient to believe that change can happen through the therapeutic process. We encourage and enhance this belief through a series of rituals and props: academic degrees, the fifty-minute hour, and so on.[20]

Jerome Frank, in his classic text *Persuasion and Healing*,[21] suggests that all nonphysical types of healing, including psychotherapy, placebos, and faith healing, rely in large part on interpersonal persuasion for their effectiveness. One of the core paradoxes in psychotherapy is that the process of interpersonal belief and persuasion that is responsible for so much of the effectiveness of psychotherapy also creates an enormous vulnerability for the patient. As therapists, we need to be particularly watchful of our overt and covert agendas.

Carl Roger originally called his work *non-directive psychotherapy* because his approach involved reflecting back to clients what they were saying, with unconditional positive regard,[22] similar to Freud's concept of an "evenly hovering attention."[23] However, using verbatim transcripts of his work, a colleague pointed out to Rogers the myriad and often subtle and unconscious ways Rogers was communicating selective approval or disapproval to his clients, which then clearly shaped what his clients did or did not talk about. For example, when Rogers nodded, or said "uh, hmm" the client was more likely to continue talking about that subject than if Rogers was silent. Similarly, Freud is said to have been distressed to learn that his patients sometimes made up dreams that fit his theories in order to please him. Accordingly, Rogers changed the name of his therapeutic approach from *non-directive* to *client-centered* psychotherapy.[24]

As a psychotherapist, I aspire to help people be more fully themselves. There are certainly times when I think I know what is best for someone else, but those are not my best days, not when I am doing my best work. Whatever agendas I have for someone else are obstacles to their change and it is my responsibility to figure out how to set those aside. There are rare occasions when a patient has an agenda that I just cannot support, or an agenda that is so personally difficult for me that I am not interested in doing the personal work to embrace. For example, I have never been sympathetic with men who are uninvolved and disinterested fathers. I work well with men who want to be more involved with and emotionally connected with their children, but I have never done well with fathers who are uninvolved and not interested in changing that. It is just too painful for me, and I cannot get past my own critical judgments. This is my limitation, not the patients', and the only ethical option is to refer those patients to another therapist.

The key to successful psychotherapy is to avoid the power struggles that inevitably result any time I have an agenda for a patient. Remember my mantra for psychotherapy: "Any patient can defeat any therapist at any time." If you will repeat this mantra on a regular basis, perhaps hourly at first, it will greatly increase your efficacy as a therapist and make you a heck of a lot happier in your work. When teaching this in workshops, I like to ask a volunteer to stand in front of the group with me, with our hands on each other's shoulders. I start to push gently on the volunteer's shoulders and he or she inevitably responds by pushing back. Back and forth we go, matching each other's escalation, each of us failing to realize that we are each choosing to face in the one and only direction that keeps us stuck. Either of us can choose at any time to turn in any other direction and the impasse is immediately undone.

The way out of this bind in psychotherapy is to step to the side, disengage from the power struggle, and collaboratively process with the patient the impasse we are in together. For example, I might say, "I notice that I have made the same suggestion to you a number of times in this session, and I've felt a little blown off each time. I know that I'm not doing my best work when I try to tell you what to do with your life, so I wonder what's going on between us that we are stuck in this place?"

Listening and Exploring

As therapists, we do not just listen; we listen in a way designed to help our patients further explore and expand their capacity to understand and embrace their experience. We do this by honoring our patients as the experts on their own lived experience and eschewing any privilege that might accrue from objectivity or professional status. We approach the narrative of our patients' experience with a naïve and courageous curiosity, like an anthropologist visiting a culture she knows nothing about.

Operationally, we listen to patients talk about their experience and we ask questions to help us understand the interiority of their experience, to understand their experience from the inside out, as if we were living the experience ourselves. When a patient says he or she feels "anxious," we do not just proceed, assuming that we know what *anxious* means. We have an idea of what the experience of anxiety is like for us, but we do not assume we know what it means for this patient in this context at this time. Our curiosity about patients' experience is courageous in that we are not afraid to sound stupid by asking questions that others might assume we should know about, or ask questions that are uncomfortable for the patient and for us to talk about: questions about sexuality, money, and so on.

As we listen, we help patients track and expand their capacity to embrace their own experience. We ask questions to help patients understand and embrace their lived experience, and avoid the mutual temptation to analyze, predict, or solve their experience. We are interested and engaged when patients talk directly about their own lived experience, and point out to our patients when they confuse derivatives for their lived experience.

Hanging in There and Tolerating Productive Tension

> The art of medicine consists of amusing the patient while nature cures the disease.
>
> —Voltaire[25]

A therapist's job is to comfort the afflicted and afflict the comfortable. The therapist's job is to tolerate the internal tension the patient brings to the relationship in order to help the patient hang in there and tolerate his or her own internal tension. The therapist brings to the endeavor her or his capacity to tolerate a broad enough range of experience, which helps the therapist to better hang in there through the vicissitudes of an intensely intimate relationship. The therapist's job is to help the patient to better tolerate the same experience. We learn an armamentarium of techniques in graduate school, which function primarily to reduce our own anxiety and inspire more confidence in our patients, which helps us hang in there.

A patient in a psychotherapy group once asked noted family therapist Carl Whitaker, "What are you doing here?" Whitaker replied, "I am here because I am the most experienced patient in the room" (R. Felder, personal communication, 1985). Our job as psychotherapists is to be the most experienced patients in the room, to embrace fully the range of experience we share with our patients, metabolize the experience and then bring that experience back into our intimate connection with our patients. You could say that psychotherapy works best when both patient and therapist learn to be more "patient," which is true in both senses of the word. If both the patient and therapist can hang in there long enough, something miraculous usually happens.

The Therapeutic Relationship

> It is one of the most beautiful compensations of this life that no man can sincerely try to help another without helping himself.
>
> —Ralph Waldo Emerson[26]

As we discussed in chapter 3, relationships are one of the most powerful tools to help us change by embracing our experience more fully. The most robust and often replicated finding in psychotherapy outcome research is that the nature of the relationship between patient and therapist is the largest factor in the effectiveness of psychotherapy. Even in the practice of medicine, the doctor-patient alliance often has a stronger effect than the medical treatment.[27] For example, when physicians spend as little as one or two minutes counseling patients about smoking cessation, it doubles the number of patients not smoking by end of the year.[28]

In metaanalyses of hundreds of outcome studies, the therapeutic relationship accounts for thirty percent of the effectiveness of psychotherapy, compared with only fifteen percent attributable to therapeutic technique. Another fifteen percent of the effectiveness of psychotherapy is attributable to placebo, and the largest piece of the effectiveness of psychotherapy, forty percent of the outcome, is attributable to "extra therapeutic variables," meaning the patient's own innate capacity to change with or without professional help.[29] This means that we spent years in graduate school studying therapeutic techniques, which account for only fifteen percent of the effectiveness of what we do, the same amount as is attributable to placebo, which we had going for us before we went to school. We can most increase the effectiveness of our work through our participation in the therapeutic relationship.

Despite these findings, graduate training in the mental health fields emphasizes acquisition of skills and knowledge, while largely neglecting the development of the person of the therapist. For example, every training program accredited by the American Psychological Association (APA) requires extensive training in "empirically supported therapeutic techniques," yet we know that the most effective therapeutic technique is not a technique at all, but the nature of the therapeutic relationship. If we took our own research seriously, we would require training in empirically supported relationship skills, such as establishing and maintaining an effective therapeutic alliance; effectively communicating empathy, genuineness, and unconditional regard; effective use of self-disclosure; management of countertransference; and the repair of impasses and ruptures in the therapeutic alliance.[30]

The essential question is, what kind of relationship can we have with patients that best facilitates their full embrace of their own experience? Freud originally conceptualized the therapeutic relationship in very personal terms. Although he endorsed therapeutic anonymity in his professional writings, in his clinical practice Freud revealed aspects of his personal life, gave advice and gifts to patients, shared meals with patients while on vacation, regularly brought his dog into the office, and analyzed his own daughter.[31,32] Freud believed that the analyst's love for the patient was an essential part of the efficacy of psychoanalysis: "Essentially one might say the cure is affected by love."[33]

At the same time, Freud was distressed that many of the members of his inner circle were indulging in sexual relationships with their patients, which was a personal and political embarrassment to Freud and the emerging field of psychotherapy. Freud also struggled personally with the intense interpersonal demands of his work with patients. Over time, Freud progressively backed off this more personal model and moved toward a less personal, more objective approach to the therapeutic relationship. While Freud's original understanding of the curative mechanism in psychotherapy was the talking cure in which the patient put experience into words and talked about it, he shifted to an understanding of the analyst's interpretations as the primary mechanism of treatment. With this shift, the locus of therapeutic effect moved from the patient to the therapist, and the relationship shifted from being personal, mutually subjective, collaborative, and intimate to being impersonal, objective, and hierarchal.[34]

This shift in Freud's work led to an ongoing split in the field of psychotherapy between the predominant impersonal objective model of the therapeutic relationship, and a more personal, mutually subjective model. Our clinical training programs, standards of practice, and codes of ethics strongly reflect the predominant objective and impersonal model of the therapeutic relationship. This bias is so strong that the more personal approaches to the therapeutic relationship are often uncritically assumed to be "unprofessional." For example, our ethical codes emphasize prohibitions against relationships that are too personal, but do not address the problems inherent in relationships that are not personal enough. Professional meetings abound with workshops on how to protect therapists from patients by maintaining appropriate therapeutic boundaries, with hardly a mention of the fact that the primary purpose of boundaries is to facilitate a therapeutic connection that will be safe for the patient. Feminist theologian Carter Heyward pointed out, "Abuse is not simply a matter of touching people wrongly. It is, as basically, a failure to make right-relation, a refusal to touch people rightly."[35]

The APA's Division of Media published an article titled "How Are Psychologists Portrayed on Screen?"[36] The article expressed concerns that fictional therapists whose actions violate the APA code of ethics are often portrayed as brilliant or even noble. The article states, "Examples include therapists played by Barbara Streisand in *Prince of Tides* and Robin Williams in *Good Will Hunting*. Both characters made great therapeutic inroads with their patients but crossed ethical boundaries in the process. . . . Williams discussed his own personal issues with his patient and at one point physically threatened him." First, there are no ethical prohibitions against therapist personal self-disclosure. Researchers like Sid Jourard have devoted their careers to demonstrating the effectiveness of therapist self-disclosure.[37] Second, the therapist played by Robin Williams actually physically assaulted his patient. Are the authors of this article actually more concerned with the therapist self-disclosing than with his assault of his patient?

The rigid adoption of an impersonal objective model for the therapeutic relationship is not based on empirically generated research, but is rather the result of an internecine political struggle. The bulk of the research supports a more personal, intersubjective model for the therapeutic relationship.[38] There are two potential relational errors in psychotherapy. These are errors of intrusion, such as offering unsolic-ited personal information about ourselves or initiating physical contact with a patient; and errors of distancing, such as refusing to provide per-sonal information about ourselves or failing to communicate empathy, genuineness, or unconditional positive regard.

The predominant clinical model holds that errors of intrusion are the cause of the majority of therapeutic failures, and that errors of distanc-ing do not substantially interfere with effective psychotherapy. As a result, clinical training programs emphasize avoiding errors of intrusion while largely ignoring errors of distancing. Our model of a well-trained therapist is one who makes the fewest mistakes rather than one who strives to be the most effective. Similarly, our professional codes of ethics impose harsh penalties for perceived errors of intrusion, while remaining silent on the matter of errors of distancing.

Contrary to the predictions of the predominant model, errors of distancing are more predictive of treatment failures than are errors of intrusion. Beginning with Strupp's landmark outcome research in the 1960s,[39] research has consistently found that errors of distancing, rather than errors of intrusion, are more predictive of bad outcome in psychotherapy.[40] In one study, eighty percent of the patients who were dissatisfied with their psychotherapy said their therapists were more likely to make an error of distancing than an error of intrusion. Of those who said they were satisfied with their psychotherapy, 90% said their therapists were more likely to make an intrusive error than an error of distancing. The patients who were dissatisfied most often reported their therapists to be distant, uninvolved, or cold.[41] Similar findings have also been reported regarding behavioral treatments[42] and psychoanalytic therapy.[43] In addition, errors of distancing create more potential for harm in psychotherapy than errors of intrusion.[44, 45]

As psychotherapists, we live out the ambivalence of this split in the field. I teach workshops around the country about a more personalized model for the therapeutic relationship, and there are always therapists who approach me after the workshop to tell me how relieved they are to hear this model legitimized because it more accurately reflects their practice. Interestingly, surveys of practicing clinicians suggest that the longer we practice, the further we move away from the impersonal, objective models of our training, and the closer we move toward a more personal, mutually subjective approach. This suggests that either therapists have become increasingly incompetent and unethical over time, or we are learning something in our clinical practices that differs significantly from the models we trained in.

Another reason we hesitate to embrace our intuitive preference for a more personal intersubjective model is the field's excessive focus on avoiding errors of intrusion in the form of relational reenactments, unconsciously recreating the relational patterns that have been most problematic to the patient. Patients often enter the therapeutic relationship fearing a recapitulation of the interpersonal injuries they have suffered in other relationships. They are often exquisitely sensitive to any of our reactions that might confirm their worst beliefs about themselves: that they are unlikable, too demanding, draining, and so on.

We certainly do not want to be a part of recreating a painful interpersonal pattern for the patient, and it is very tempting to try to avoid the whole situation by maintaining a certain emotional distance and attempting to conceal any of our emotional or personal reactions that might harm the patient. The problem with this approach is that much more is known in an intimate exchange than just what is said. As mentioned earlier in this chapter, only twenty percent of what we understand from another person's communication comes from the words spoken.[46]

When a patient asks, "Are you angry with me?" our reflexive response is to deny it before we even know if it is true, or to fall back on a standard therapeutic dodge such as, "Why do you think I am angry with you?" We do not like to think of ourselves as being angry with a patient; after all, we are there to help. We are supposed to be the better symbolic parent, the one who does not hurt the patient. Even when we realize we are angry with the patient, we conjure up a clinical rationale for blaming the patient for our anger rather than looking at our own part of the interaction. The patient is left to believe either that his or her experience is on target and the therapist is being dishonest, or that he or she cannot trust his or her own internal experience. The formula to make someone crazy is to use a hierarchically superior position to undermine consistently his or her experience of the world.

I was working with a young woman who was telling me about her recent engagement. As I listened, I was surprised to notice my lack of excitement, although we had spoken often of her desire to marry this young man. I considered the possibility that I was being cold-hearted; perhaps I was not excited because I did not care as much about this young woman as I thought. I decided to share my confusion with her. She sat silently for a while, and then began to sob deeply. What emerged was that she too had not been feeling as excited by the event as she had anticipated, and she began to understand the ways in which she habitually suppressed her excitement, having been taught early in life that too much open emotional expression made others (i.e., her family) feel uncomfortable.

We cannot avoid relational reenactments in psychotherapy; it is like trying not to marry your mother or your father. We all replay our core interpersonal patterns in our intimate relationships. That is what makes the relationships intimate. All of us reenact our relational issues. Heinz Kohut said that empathic failures are the gold mines of psychotherapy.[47] Finding yourself in the middle of a painful relational reenactment with a patient gives you the opportunity to work collaboratively with the patient toward a more satisfying outcome.

Intimacy in the Therapeutic Relationship

In chapter 3, I suggested that intimate relationships hold the most potential for in-depth and enduring characterological change. While research supports the efficacy of a more personal intersubjective model for the therapeutic relationship, the notion of the therapeutic relationship as an intimate relationship has been unsettling since the inception of the field. There is a lot of literature in the field on warmth and empathy and numerous warnings against over-involvement with patients, but very little has been written on intimacy or love in the therapeutic relationship.[48] When surveyed, therapists said that the emotion they were most comfortable sharing with patients was anger, and the emotion they were least comfortable sharing with a patient was warmth or affection.[49]

Intimacy is the capacity to be you while in relationship with someone else.[50] As psychotherapists, we participate in an intimate relationship with our patients by being more fully ourselves in the relationship. We help our patients embrace the full range of their experience by more fully embracing the range of our own experience. From an intrapsychic perspective, focusing on your own experience detracts from being able to connect with someone else. From a relational perspective, however, the more fully you embrace your own experience the more intimate you can be with others. As one of my teachers, Earl Brown, said, "What is apt to be impactful with someone, is someone else being themselves with you, which then encourages you to be yourself with them."[51] Feminist psychologist Judy Jordan made the point more forcefully, saying that a "relationship cannot be growth enhancing for one person if it is not growth enhancing for both."[52]

Participating in a more personal, intimate relationship with our patients is not as simple as being more self-disclosing. Historical self-disclosure, in particular, is not conducive to increased intimacy in the therapeutic relationship.[53] An intimate connection is an internal connection, a connection at the level of lived experience. Sharing a piece of historical information, such as "I am in recovery," is no guarantee of embracing the internal experience the patient is talking about. You do not need to have lived through the same kinds of things that your patients are going through in order to understand them. It is being willing to embrace more fully your own internal experience that helps others. Maybe you did not grow up with the same kind of academic and peer pressure that your kids are facing, but if you are willing to embrace your own fears of failure and your loneliness and doubts about yourself, then you can really be of help. I love the old saying, "Let me give you some advice, because I'm not using it."

I have worked with combat veterans for many years, and while veterans are notorious for rejecting therapists who have not themselves served in combat, veterans rarely challenge me on this point. I believe that is because I don't pretend to understand the external experience they have been though, but I am well acquainted with my own internal rage, enough to have often wondered what it would have been like if I had been set loose in a "free-fire zone" with an automatic weapon at the age of nineteen.

Therapeutic intimacy involves locating the experience the patient is struggling to embrace within yourself, and then bringing that experience back into your relationship with the patient. There is a story about a woman traveling a great distance with her son to visit Mahatma Gandhi. When she arrived in front of the great man, she asked Gandhi to tell her son to stop eating sugar. Gandhi asked them to come back in three days. When they returned, Gandhi asked the young man to stop eating sugar.

Grateful, yet puzzled, the woman asked Gandhi why he had not simply told the young man this three days earlier. Gandhi replied, "Three days ago I was still eating sugar."[54]

Mutuality in the Therapeutic Relationship

From a relational perspective, the ideal relationship is one of mutuality, "a way of being connected with one another in such a way that both, or all, of us are empowered . . . [and] able to be ourselves at our best."[55] Rather than thinking of relationships in win-lose terms, mutuality suggests that a relationship can only be growth enhancing for one person when it is growth enhancing for both. In mutuality, there is an open exchange between people, with each providing the stimulus for growth in the other, an alchemy in which both are changed. Jung wrote, "The meeting of two personalities is like the contact of two chemical substances: if there is any reaction, both are transformed."[56]

Mutuality requires the capacity to attend to the experience of others, while simultaneously remaining aware of our own experience. Each person must be able to both join and separate, to take both a subjective and an objective position, to function as both an experiencing self and an observing self. If the balance shifts excessively toward separation in a relationship, then there will not be sufficient joining for intimacy. If the balance shifts too much toward joining in a relationship, then there will not be enough separateness for intimacy.[57] Most intimate relationships move back and forth over time, with both people seeking a balance that works for them.

The opposite of mutuality is projection. Mutuality requires the capacity to accept responsibility for our own experience rather than blaming the alleged shortcoming of others for any relational impasse. In striving toward mutuality, each person seeks to understand and embrace the other's experience as it lives within himself or herself, embracing the differences rather than merely tolerating them. The willingness to engage in this struggle, the interpenetration of character by relationship, is what makes intimate relationships the most potentially powerful vehicle for personal change.[58] Mutuality is what makes the difference between a relationship that is mutually enhancing and one that can be mutually destructive.

It is particularly important for therapists to bring our vulnerability, our own woundedness, to the therapeutic encounter. Carl Jung wrote,

"Only the wounded physician heals. But when the doctor wears his personality like a coat of armor, he has no effect."[59] Theologian Henri Nouwen wrote, "No one can help anyone without becoming involved, without entering with his whole person into the painful situation, without taking the risk of becoming hurt, wounded, or even destroyed in the process. Who can take away suffering without entering it?"[60]

As therapists, we sometimes avoid the potential depth of a more intimate connection with our patients because of our reluctance to embrace fully our own experience. Sometimes we are afraid of the impact of joining with another in the depths of his or her experience. There is a lot of concern among therapists about burnout, and a general belief that therapists burn out by getting too close to their patients' experiences, too close with their patients. It is my belief, however, that therapist burnout is the result of the energy drain of keeping oneself distant from someone else's powerful experience, and that intimacy in the therapeutic relationship, or any relationship, is the best protection against burnout.

The psychotherapeutic relationship, like all other intimate relationships, is primarily an unconscious relationship. Like lovers, therapist and patient are drawn to each other by our unrecognized needs. We unconsciously draw patients to us who are working on whatever issues we are currently wrestling with ourselves. In fact, experiential authors suggest that therapists retire when they no longer need to do psychotherapy to help them with their own growth.[61]

One of the best parts of being a psychotherapist is that patients come to us to work on the issues that are the most personally challenging in our own lives, and one of the worst parts about being a psychotherapist is that patients come to us to work on the issues that are the most personally challenging in our own lives. If you can see this process as a challenge, and as an opportunity for growth, then being in an intimate therapeutic relationship is exhilarating and expansive. If you see this process as an intrusion to defend against, then being in an intimate therapeutic relationship is perpetually frustrating and draining.

When we attempt to remove intimacy from the therapeutic relationship, when we strive to manualize the therapeutic relationship into a fee-for-service business relationship, we risk stripping away the core effectiveness of our work. Not talking about intimacy in psychotherapy does not make the issue go away; it just drives it underground. For example, seventy-five percent of therapists acknowledged being sexually attracted to some patients, but a large majority said they would never consider discussing those feelings with a supervisor or colleague.[62] As therapists, surely we understand that any issue you do not address directly is more likely to be unconsciously acted out. Susan Bauer, in her courageous book *The Intimate Hour*,[63] suggests that our failure to address directly the issue of intimacy in the therapeutic relationship contributes directly to the incidence of sexual acting out by therapists.

NOTES

FROG AND TOAD: THE GARDEN

1. Lobel, A. (1999). *Frog and Toad Together.* New York: Harper Festival.
2. Ibid.

PREFACE

1. Popper, K. (2002). *The open society and its enemies: The spell of plato.* New York: Psychology Press, p. 138.
2. Lewis, C. D. *The Poetic Image.* Quoted in Shilling, L., & Fuller, L. (1997). *Dictionary of Quotations in Communications.* Westport, CT: Greenwood Publishing Group, p. 164.
3. Weiss, A. (1986). *The patient's experience of privacy in psychotherapy* (Doctoral dissertation, Georgia State University).
4. Based on surveys of therapists in workshops across the country.
5. U.S. Census data. Retrieved from http://ecp3113-01.fa01.fsu.edu/lively_introduction/Migration.htm#box3.
6. Williams, B., Sawyer, S., & Wahlstrom, C. (2005). *Marriages, families & intimate relationships: A practical introduction.* New York: Allyn & Bacon.
7. Felder, R., & Weiss, A. (1992). *Experiential psychotherapy: A symphony of selves.* Lanham, MD: University of America Press.

NOTES TO CHAPTER 1

1. Zubko, A. (2000). *Treasury of spiritual wisdom: A collection of 10,000 powerful quotations for transforming your life.* New Delhi, India: Motilal Banarsidass, p. 475.

2. Chang, L. (2006). *Wisdom for the soul: Five millenia of prescriptions for spiritual healing.* Washington, DC: Gnosophia Publishers, p. 117.

3. Hubble, M., Duncan, B. & Miller, S. (2003). *The heart and soul of change: What works in therapy.* Washington, D.C.: American Psychological Association

4. Prochaska, J., Norcross, J., & DiClemente, C. (1995). *Changing for good: A revolutionary six-stage program for overcoming bad habits and moving your life positively forward.* New York: Harper Paperbacks.

5. Deutschman, A. (2007). *Change or die: The three keys to change at work and in life.* New York: Harper Collins.

6. Polivy, J., & Herman, P. (2002). If at first you don't succeed: False hopes of self-change. *American Psychologist, 57*(9), 677–689.

7. Morris, D. (1967). *The naked ape: A zoologists study of the human animal.* New York: Delta Books.

8. Fadiman, J. (2005, February). Dare to dream. *Woman's Day Magazine,* 62.

9. *Hebrew-English Tanakh,* student edition. (2000). Jewish Publication Society of America, Exodus 14:13–14.

10. Hubble, M., Duncan, B. & Miller, S. (2003). *The heart and soul of change: What works in therapy.*

11. Palmer, T. H. (1840). *Teacher's manual.* p. 223.

12. Roosevelt, F. (1933). *Looking forward.* Whitefish, MT: Kessinger, p. 31.

13. Burns, R. (1786). *Country: To a mouse, on turning her up in her nest with the plough.* Published in The Kilmarnock Volume by John Wilson.

14. Beck, M. (2008, January). Know when to fold 'em. *Oprah Magazine,* 47–49.

15. Arkes, H., & Blumer, C. (1985). The psychology of sunk cost. *Organizational Behavior and Human Decision Process, 35,* 124–140.

16. Prochaska, J., Norcross, J., & DiClemente, C. (1995). *Changing for good: A revolutionary six-stage program for overcoming bad habits and moving your life positively forward.* New York: Harper Paperbacks.

17. Taggart, C. (2011). *An apple a day: Old-fashioned proverbs—timeless words to live by.* New York: Penguin, p. 76.

18. Coburn, P. (2006). *The change function: Why some technologies take off and others crash and burn.* New York: Penguin, p. 174.

19. Bowden, M. (2007). *Guests of the Ayatolla: The Iran hostage crisis: The first battle in America's war with militant Islam.* New York: Grove Press.

20. Nouwen, H. (1996). *Bread for the journey: A daybook of wisdom and faith*. New York: Harper One, p. 67.

21. Hubble, M., Duncan, B. & Miller, S. (2003). *The heart and soul of change: What works in therapy.*

22. Ibid.

23. Ibid.

24. Ibid.

25. Talbort, M. (2000, January 9). The placebo prescription. *New York Times.*

26. AA Services. (2007). *Alcoholics Anonymous: Big book*, 1st ed. Alcoholics Anonymous World Services.

27. Hubble, M., Duncan, B. & Miller, S. (2003). *The heart and soul of change: What works in therapy.*

NOTES TO CHAPTER 2

1. Hubble, M., Duncan, B. & Miller, S. (2003). *The heart and soul of change: What works in therapy*. Washington, D.C.: American Psychological Association.

2. Husserl, E. (1931/1960). *Cartesisan meditations: An introduction to phenomenology*. Cairns, D. (Trans.). Martinus Nijhoff.

3. Stern, D. (2000). *The interpersonal world of the infant: A view from psychoanalysis and developmental psychology*. New York: Basic Books.

4. Hubble, M., Duncan, B. & Miller, S. (2003). *The heart and soul of change: What works in therapy.*

5. Bolt, B. (2006). *Earthquakes*, 5th ed. New York: W.H. Freeman and Company.

6. AA Services. (2007). *Alcoholics Anonymous: Big Book*, 1st ed. Alcoholics Anonymous World Services.

7. Coe, F. (Producer), & Pen, A. (Director). (1962). *The miracle worker* [Motion picture]. USA: Playfilm Productions.

8. Thoreau, H. D. (2008). *Life without principle*. Charleston, SC: Forgotten Books.

9. Fragment 41, quoted by Plato in *Cratylus.*

10. Simpson, J., & Weiner, E. (1989). *The Oxford English Dictionary*. Oxford University Press.

11. Csíkszentmihályi, M. (1996). *Creativity: Flow and the psychology of discovery and invention*. New York: Harper Perennial.

12. Tribole, E., & Resch, E. (2003). *Intuitive eating: A revolutionary program that works*. New York: St. Martin's Griffin, p. 56.

13. Bishop, P. (1999). *Jung in contexts: A reader.* London: Psychology Press, p. xvi.

14. Rogers, C. R., Kirschenbaum, H., & Henderson, V. (1989). *The Carl Rogers reader.* New York: Houghton Mifflin Harcourt, p. 19.

15. Zedong, M. & Knight, N. (1990). *Mao Zedong on dialectical materialism.* Armonk, NY: M.E. Sharpe, p. 138.

16. Wolpe, J. (1958). *Psychotherapy by reciprocal inhibition.* Stanford: Stanford University Press.

17. Chang, L. *Wisdom for the soul: Five millenia of prescriptions for spiritual healing.* Washington, DC: Gnosophia Publishers, p. 64.

18. Bateson, M. C. (2010). *Willing to learn: Passages of personal discovery.* London: Steerforth.

19. Nichols, M. (Producer & Director). (1990). *Postcards from the edge* [Motion picture]. USA: Columbia Pictures Corporation.

20. Smith, E. L. (2003). *The person of the therapist.* Jefferson, NC: McFarland, p. 118.

21. Orloff, J. (2009). *Emotional freedom: Liberate yourself from negative emotions and transform your life.* New York: Harmony Press.

22. Hong, L., & Page, S. (2000, February 17). Problem solving by heterogeneous agents. *The Journal of Economic Theory,* 1–39.

23. Niebuhr, R. (1934). *The serenity prayer.*

24. Fisher-McGarry, J. & Robbins, J. *Be the change you want to see in the world: 365 things you can do for yourself and your planet.* Berkeley, CA: Conari Press, p. 89.

25. Hubble, M., Duncan, B. & Miller, S. (2003). *The heart and soul of change: What works in therapy.*

26. Ibid., p. 279.

27. Ibid., p. 233.

28. Higgins, E. (2008, June/July). The new genetics of mental illness. *Scientific American Mind,* pp. 41–47.

29. Nell, J., & Kniskern, D. (1989). *From psyche to system: The evolving therapy of Carl Whitaker.* New York: The Guildford Press.

30. Agel, J. (1971). *The radical therapist: The radical therapist collective.* New York: Ballentine Books.

31. New King James Version Holy Bible. (2006). Thomas Nelson.

32. Maturana, H., & Varela, F. (1988). *The tree of knowledge.* New Science Library, Shambhala, Boston, p. 242.

33. *Hebrew-English Tanakh,* Student Edition, (2000). Jewish Publication Society of America, Genesis 1:3.

34. Carrere, R.A. (1992). Psychoanalysis as talking cure: The problem of the patient's reality. *Modern Psychoanalysis,* 27(1), p. 63.

35. Lieberman, M. (2003). Does rejection hurt? An FMRI study of social exclusion. *Science, 302*(5643), pp. 290–292.

36. Pennebaker, J. (2002). *Emotion, disclosure and health.* Washington, D.C.: American Psychological Association.

37. Pennebaker, J., & Susman, J. R. (1988). Disclosure of traumas and psychosomatic processes. *Social Science and Medicine, 26,* pp. 327–332.

38. Pennebaker, J. (1997). *Opening up: The healing power of expressing emotions.* New York: Guilford Press.

39. Levitt, J., & Straffeld, M. (2000). *A night of questions.* Elkins Park, PA: Reconstructionist Press, Exodus 13:8.

NOTES TO CHAPTER 3

1. Homish, G., & Leonard, K. (2005). Spousal influence on smoking behaviors in a US community sample of newly married couples. *Social Science Medicine, 61,* pp. 2557–2567.

2. Psychotherapy: Theory, research, practice and training. (2001, Winter). *Special Issue: Empirically Supported Therapy Relationships: Summary Report of the Division 29 Task Force, 29*(4).

3. Hubble, M., Duncan, B. & Miller, S. (2003). *The heart and soul of change: What works in therapy.* Washington, D.C.: American Psychological Association.

4. Ibid., p. 301.

5. Wang, H., Mittleman, M., Leineweber, C., & Orth-Gomer, K. (2006). Depressive symptoms, social isolation, and progression of coronary artery atherosclerosis: The Stockholm female coronary angiography study. *Psychotherapy and Psychosomatics, 75*(2), pp. 96–102.

6. Wilson, R., Krueger, K., Arnold, S., Schneider, J., Kelly, J., Barnes, L., Tang, Y., & Bennett, D. (2007). Loneliness and risk of Alzheimer's disease. *Archives of General Psychiatry, 64*(2), pp. 234–240.

7. Hubble, M., Duncan, B. & Miller, S. (2003). *The heart and soul of change: What works in therapy.*

8. Bove, C., Soval, B., & Rauschenbach, B. (2003). Food choices among newly married couples: convergence, conflict, individualism, and projects. *Appetite, 40*(1), 25–41.

9. Ross, L. (1977). The intuitive psychologist and his shortcomings: Distortions in the attribution Process. In L. Berkowitz (Ed.). *Advances in experimental social psychology* (Vol 10, pp. 173–220). New York: Academic Press.

10. Greenberg, S. (2005). *Wrestling with God: Homosexuality in the Jewish tradition*. Madison: University of Wisconsin Press.

11. Ellenberger, H. (1970). *The discovery of the unconscious: The history and evolution of dynamic psychiatry*. New York: Basic Books.

12. Jordan, J. (1989). *A relational approach to psychotherapy*. Paper presented at the annual meeting of the Georgia Psychological Association. Atlanta, GA.

13. Jordan, J., Kaplan, A., Miller, J., Stiver, I., & Surrey, J. (1991). *Women's growth in connection: Writings from the Stone Center*. New York: Guilford Press.

14. Jung, C. G.(1955). *Modern man in search of a soul*. New York: Harcourt Harvest, p. 49.

15. Gilligan, C. (1982). *In a different voice: Psychological theory and women's development*. Boston: Harvard University Press.

16. Buber, M. (2010). *I and thou*. Eastford, CT: Martino Fine Books.

17. Rosenthal, R., & Jacobson, L. (1992). *Pygmalion in the classroom*. New York: Irvington.

18. Aesop. (1990). The wind and the sun. In *Aesop's fables: A classic illustrated edition*. San Francisco: Chronicle Books.

19. Ross, W. D. (2010). *Aristotle*. New York: Cosimo, Inc, p. 7.

20. Rempel, L., & Rempel, J. (2004). Partner influence on health behavior decision-making: Increasing breast-feeding duration. *Journal of Social and Personal Relationships, 21*(1), 92–111.

21. Frank, J. (1991). *Persuasion and healing*. Baltimore, MD: Johns Hopkins Press.

22. Rosenthal, D. (1955). Change in some moral values following psychotherapy. *Journal of Consulting Psychology, 19*(6), 431–436.

23. Bright, I., Baker, K., & Neimeyer, R. (1999). Professional and paraprofessional group treatments for depression: A comparison of cognitive-behavioral and mutual support interventions. *Journal of Consulting and Clinical Psychology, 67*(4), 491–501.

24. Graham, H. (1999). Help or hindrance? An examination of the effectiveness of children's grief support groups. *Dissertation Abstracts International Section A: Humanities and Social Sciences, 60*(6-A), 2227.

25. Cummings, S., Long, J., Peterson-Hazan, S., & Harrison, J. (1998). The efficacy of a group treatment model in helping spouses meet the emotional and practical challenges of early stage care-giving. *Clinical Gerontologist, 20*(1), 29–45.

26. Rowe, M., Bellamy, C., Baranoski, M., Wieland, M., O'Connell, M., Benedict, P., Davidson, L., Buchanan, J., & Sells, D. (2007). A peer-support, group intervention to reduce substance use and criminality among persons with severe mental illness. *Psychiatric Services, 58*(7), 955–961.

27. Durkheim, E. (1997). *Suicide*. New York: Free Press.

28. Georgetown University Medical Center. (2011, April 4). Social isolation, stress-induced obesity increases breast cancer risk in mice. *ScienceDaily*. Retrieved June 26, 2011, from http://www.sciencedaily.com /releases/2011/04/110404131453 .htm.

29. Hubble, M., Duncan, B. & Miller, S. (2003). *The heart and soul of change: What works in therapy*.

30. Weiss, A. G. (2002). The lost role of dependency in psychotherapy. *Gestalt Review*, 6(1), 6–17.

31. Ibid.

32. Guntrip, H. (1969). *Schizoid phenomena: Object relations and the self*. New York: Basic Books.

33. Nin, A. (1967). *The diary of Anais Nin*, Volume 2: 1934–1939. New York: The Swallow Press.

34. Chopra, D. (1998). *The path to love: Spiritual strategies for healing*. Google e-Book, p. 4.

35. Malone, T., & Malone, P. (1988). *Art of intimacy*. Los Angeles: Fireside.

36. Attenborough, R. (Director). (1982). *Gandhi* [Motion picture]. United Kingdom & India: International Film Investors.

37. Shakespeare, W. (2003). *Hamlet*. New York: Simon & Schuster/The New Folger Shakespeare Library, Act 3, Scene 2, Line 254.

38. Tillich, P. (1969). *The Shaking of the Foundations*. New York: Penguin.

39. Pennebaker, J. (2002). *Emotion, disclosure and health*. Washington, D.C.: American Psychological Association.

NOTES TO CHAPTER 4

1. Heraclitus, quoted in *Lives of the Philosophers* by Diogenes Laërtius. (1969). Chicago: Regnery.

2. Grothe, M. (2009). *Ifferisms: An anthology of aphorisms that begin with the word "if."* New York: Harper Collins, p. 101.

3. Thoreau, H. D. (2007). *The journal of Thoreau*. Volume 10, August 1857 to June 1958. Salt Lake City: Peregrine Smith Books/UT.

4. Ibid.

5. Jourard, S. M. (1981). *The transparent self*. New York: Van Nostrand, p. 64.

6. Hubble, M., Duncan, B. & Miller, S. (2003). *The heart and soul of change: What works in therapy*. Washington, D.C.: American Psychological Association.

7. Blakeslee, S. (2005). This is your brain under hypnosis. *New York Times*, science section, pp. 3–5, 11/22/05.

8. Arndt, B. (1986). *Private lives.* New York: Penguin, p. 145.

9. Emerson, R. W. (2010). *Self-reliance.* Seattle, WA: Create Space, p. 54.

10. Bridges, W. (2010). *Managing transitions: Making the most of change.* Readhowyouwant.com, p. 89.

11. Malhotra, M. (2005). *Orient book of quotations.* Quotationsbook.com, p. 90.

12. New Oxford American Dictionary. (2010). New York: Oxford University Press.

13. AA Services. (2007). *Alcoholics Anonymous: Big book,* 1st ed. Alcoholics Anonymous World Services.

14. Shaw, G. B. (2010). *Man and superman: A comedy and a philosophy.* IndoEuropeanPubishing.com, p. 27.

15. Frankl, V. (2006). *Man's search for meaning.* Boston: Beacon Press.

16. Lama, D., & Mehrotra, R. (2006). *The essential Dalai Lama: His important teachings.* New York: Penguin, p. 197.

17. Polivy, J., & Herman, P. (2002). If at first you don't succeed: False hopes of self-change. *American Psychologist, 57*(9), 677–689.

18. Lennon, J. (1980). Beautiful boy (darling boy). On *Double Fantasy* [CD].

19. Arieti, S. (1978). On schizophrenia, phobias depression, psychotherapy and the farther shores of psychiatry: Selected papers of Silvano Arieti. New York: Brouner-Routledge.

20. Weiss, A. G. (1986). *The patient's experience of privacy in psychotherapy* (Unpublished doctoral dissertation). Georgia State University, pp. 124–127.

21. Bettleheim, B. (1980). *Surviving and other essays.* New York: Vintage, p. 23.

22. D'Haenen, H. A. H., den Boer, J., & Wilner, P. (Eds.). *Biological psychiatry,* vol 1. New York: Wiley.

23. Epstein, S. (1991). The self-concept, the traumatic neurosis, and the structure of personality. In D. Ozer, J. M. Healy, Jr., & A. J. Stewart (Eds.). *Perspectives in personality.* London: Jessica Kingsley Publishers, Ltd.

24. Janoff-Buhlman, R. (2002). *Shattered assumptions.* New York: Free Press.

25. Haynes, S. (1991). *Prospects for post-Holocaust theology.* Atlanta, GA: American Academy of Religion.

26. Wiesel, E. (1995). *The trial of God.* New York: Schocken.

27. Ibid.

28. Lifton, R. J. (2005). *Home from the war: Learning from Vietnam veterans.* Boston: Other Press.

29. Anderson, H. C. (author), Burton, V. (illustrator). (2004). *The Emperor's New Clothes.* Sandpiper.

30. Cleland, M. (2000) *Strong at the broken places.* Lanham, MD: Taylor Trade Publishing.

NOTES TO CHAPTER 5

1. Dalfen, A. (2008). *When baby brings the blues: Solutions for postpartum depression.* New York: John Wiley and Sons, p. 231.

2. Prochaska, J., Norcorss, J., & DiClemente, C. (1995). *Changing for good: A revolutionary six-stage program for overcoming bad habits and moving your life positively forward.* New York: Harper Paperbacks.

3. Levitt, E. E. (1980). *The psychology of anxiety,* 2nd ed. New Jersey: Lawrence Erlbaum Associates.

4. Deane, D. (2007). *Honor your gifts.* Longwood, FL: Xulon Press, p. 49.

5. Freud, S., & Strachey, J. (1989), *Introductory lectures on psychoanalysis.* New York: Liveright, Standard Edition, 16:357.

6. Spitz, R. (1965). Hospitalism. An inquiry into the genesis of psychiatric conditions in early childhood. In *The Psychoanalytic Study of the Child (1945): The First Year of Life. A Psychoanalytic Study of Normal and Deviant Development of Object Relations.* New York, International Universities Press, Inc., pp. 277–278.

7. Freud, S., & Strachey, J. *Introductory lectures.*

8. Mencken, H. L. (1942). *A new dictionary of quotations on historical principles from ancient and modern sources.* New York: A. A. Knopf.

9. Kramer, P. (2002). Is it time for a change? *Woman's Day, 65*(12), 64–70.

10. Levitt, E. E. *The psychology of anxiety.*

11. Moncrieff, J. (1999) An investigation into the precedents of modern drug treatment in psychiatry. *History of Psychiatry, 10,* 475–490.

12. Mojtabai, R. (2009). *Psychiatric Services, 60*(August), 1015–1023.

13. Hubble, M., Duncan, B. & Miller, S. (2003). *The heart and soul of change: What works in therapy.* Washington, D.C.: American Psychological Association.

14. Ibid., p. 307.

NOTES TO CHAPTER 6

1. Calvin cited in Wormeli, R. (2003). *Day one and beyond.* Portland, ME: Stenhouse, p. 177.

2. Hubble, M., Duncan, B. & Miller, S. (2003). *The Heart and Soul of Change-What Works in Therapy.* Washington, D.C.: American Psychological Association.

3. Ibid., p. 250.

4. Demosthenes, 338 B.C.

5. Resch, E. & Tribole, E. (2003). *Intuitive eating: A revolutionary program that works.* New York: St. Martins Griffin.

6. Prochaska, J. O., Norcross, J. C., & DiClemente, C. C. (1994). *Changing for good: The revolutionary program that explains the six stages of change and teaches you how to free yourself from bad habits.* New York: W. Morrow, p. 251.

7. Words of wisdom: For some people, optimistic thoughts can do more harm than good. *The Economist,* July 11, 2009.

8. Prochaska, Norcross, & DiClemente, p. 16.

9. Ibid., p. 182.

10. Gladwell, M. (2005). *Blink: The power of thinking without thinking.* New York: Little, Brown and Co.

11. Robbins, T. (1990). *Skinny legs and all.* New York: Bantam.

12. Mermelstein, D., personal communication, 2005.

13. Keyes, K. (1984). *The hundredth monkey.* Los Angeles: Devorss and Company.

NOTES TO CHAPTER 7

1. Mahatma Gandhi, as quoted in Potts, M. W. (2002, Feb. 1). Arun Gandhi shares the Mahatma's message. *India-West,* 27(13), p. A34.

2. Hubble, M., Duncan, B. & Miller, S. (2003). *The heart and soul of change: What works in therapy.* Washington, D.C.: American Psychological Association.

3. Frank, J. (1961). *Persuasion and healing: A comparative study of psychotherapy.* Baltimore: Johns Hopkins Press, p. 225.

4. Widener, C. (2010). *The angel inside: Michelangelo's secrets for following your passion and finding the work you love.* New York: Crown Publishing.

5. Benton, R. (Director). (2007). *Feast of love* [Motion picture]. United States: GreeneStreet Films.

6. Hempton, G. (2009). *One square inch of silence: One man's search for natural silence in a noisy world.* New York: Free Press.

7. Egan, G. (2009). *The skilled helper.* New York: Brooks Cole.

8. Gray, J. (1992). *Men are from Mars, women are from Venus.* New York: Harper Collins.

9. Mehrabian, A. & Wiener, M. (1967). Decoding of inconsistent communications. *Journal of Personality and Social Psychology.* 6(1), 109–114.

10. Prochaska, J. O., Norcross, J. C., & DiClemente, C. C. (1994). *Changing for good: The revolutionary program that explains the six stages of change and teaches you how to free yourself from bad habits.* New York: W. Morrow, p. 17.

11. Hubble, M., Duncan, B. & Miller, S. (2003). *The heart and soul of change: What works in therapy.*

12. Carrere, R. (1992). Psychoanalysis as talking cure: The problem of the patient's reality. *Modern Psychoanalysis.* 17(1), 53–67.

13. Ibid.

14. Herman, J. (1997). *Trauma and recovery.* New York: Basic Books.

15. Carrere, R. (1992). Psychoanalysis as talking cure: The problem of the patient's reality.

16. Ibid.

17. Herman, J. (1997). *Trauma and recovery.*

18. Ibid.

19. Adler, A. (2010). *Understanding human nature.* Eastford, CT: Martino Fine Books.

20. Frank, J. (1978). *Persuasion and healing.* Shockton.

21. Ibid.

22. Rogers, C. (2003). *Client-centered therapy.* London: Constable.

23. Freud, S. & Strachey, J. (1989). *Introductory lecture on psychoanalysis.* New York: Liveright, Standard Edition.

24. Kramer, R. (1995). The birth of client-centered therapy. *Journal of Humanistic Psychology.* 35(4), 54–110.

25. Rosenow, E. (2003). *The art of living . . . The art of medicine. The wit and wisdom of life and medicine: A physician's perspective.* Bloomington, IN: Trafford Publishing, p. 49.

26. Change, L. (2006). *Wisdom for the soul.* Washington, D.C.: Gnosophia.

27. Hubble, M., Duncan, B. & Miller, S. (2003). *The heart and soul of change: What works in therapy.*

28. Prochaska, J.O., Norcross, J.C., & DiClemente, C.C. (1994). *Changing for good: A revolutionary six-stage program for overcoming bad habits and moving your life positively forward.* New York: Harper. p. 62.

29. Norcorss, J. (ed.). Special Issue: Empirically Supported Therapy Relationships: Summary Report of the Division 29 Task Force. *Psychotherapy: Theory, Research, Practice and Training.* (1992). 29(4).

30. Ibid.

31. Carrere, R. (1992). Psychoanalysis as talking cure: The problem of the patient's reality.

32. Baur, S. (1997). *The intimate hour.* New York: Houghton Mifflin.

33. Covington, C. (ed.) and Wharton, B. (2003). *Sabina Spielrein: Forgotten pioneer of psychoanalysis.* New York: Routledge.

34. Carrere, R. (1992). Psychoanalysis as talking cure: The problem of the patient's reality.

35. Heyward, C. (1993). *When boundaries betray us: Beyond illusions of what is ethical in therapy and life.* San Francisco: HarperSanFrancisco.

36. How are psychologists portrayed on screen? (1998, November). *APA Monitor.*

37. Jourard, S. (1964). *The transparent self: Self-disclosure and well-being.* Princeton, N.J.: Van Nostrand.

38. Dalenberg, C. (2000). *Counter-transference and the treatment of trauma.* Washington, D.C.: American Psychological Association.

39. Strupp, H. (1993). The Vanderbuilt psychotherapy studies: Synopsis. *Journal of Consulting and Clinical Psychology.* 61(3), 431–433.

40. Dalenberg, C. (2000). *Counter-transference and the treatment of trauma.*

41. Ibid.

42. Ibid.

43. Ibid.

44. Strupp, H. (1993). The Vanderbuilt psychotherapy studies: Synopsis

45. Dalenberg, C. (2000). *Counter-transference and the treatment of trauma.*

46. Mehrabian, A. & Wiener, M. (1967). Decoding of inconsistent communications.

47. *Psychological abstracts.* (1996). Washington, D.C.: American Psycological Association.

48. Baur, S. (1997). *The intimate hour.*

49. Dalenberg, C. (2000). *Counter-transference and the treatment of trauma.*

50. Malone, T. P. (1987). *The art of intimacy.* New York: Prentice Hall.

51. Malone, K., Malone, T., Kuckleburg, R., Cox, R. Barnett, J. & Barstow, D. (1982). Experiential psychotherapy: Basic principles. *Pilgrimage.* 10(1), 1–63

52. Baker, J., Jordan, J., Stiver, I. & Surrey, J. (1991). *Women's growth in connection: Writing from the Stone Center.* New York: Guilford Press.

53. Whitaker, C. & Malone, T. (1981). *The roots of psychotherapy.* New York: Brunner/Mazel.

54. Felder, R., & Weiss, A. (1992) *Experiential psychotherapy: A symphony of selves.* Lanham, MD: University Press of America.

55. Baker, J., Jordan, J., Stiver, I. & Surrey, J. (1991). *Women's growth in connection: Writing from the Stone Center.*

56. Gilligan, S. & Simon, D. (2004). *Walking in two worlds: The relational self in theory, practice and community.* Phoenix, AZ: Zeig, Tucker & Theison.

57. Baker, J., Jordan, J., Stiver, I. & Surrey, J. (1991). *Women's growth in connection: Writing from the Stone Center.*

58. Malone, K., Malone, T., Kuckleburg, R., Cox, R. Barnett, J. & Barstow, D. (1982). Experiential psychotherapy: Basic principles.

59. Dunne, C. (2002). *Carl Jung*. New York: Continuum International Publishers.

60. Nouwen, H. (1979). *The wounded healer*. New York: Doubleday. p. 79.

61. Whitaker, C. & Malone, T. (1981). *The roots of psychotherapy*. New York: Brunner/Mazel.

62. Baur, S. (1997). *The intimate hour*.

63. Ibid.

INDEX

alcohol and drug use, 27–28, 31, 73–76, 90

backlash, 13, 39, 93, 104, 108

change: is change natural, 3–4; and the culture, xvi, 2–3, 62, 84–85, 90–91; external and internal, 2–3; in mild current, 112–13; in moderate current, 113–15; resistance to, 69, 87–88, 100–4 vs. stability, 3–4; in strong current, 104, 115–16; systemic, 43, 46–47, 85; through experience, 29–34. *See also* relationships

couples, 12, 33–34, 54, 70, 82, 123

dating: Not Trying So Hard, 14, 17–18, 19–21; Trying Harder, 8–10, 21–22

dependency and independence, 56, 61–63. *See also* psychotherapy

derivatives, 77–78; habits, 72–77; judgments, 80–82; predictions, 79–80; relational model, 70–71; trauma, 82–85

drug use. *See* alcohol and drug use

eating healthily, 13, 36, 59, 76, 103–4

embracing experience, 26–48; knowing what you know, 47–48; making room for experience, 41–43; by Not Trying So Hard, 36–38; paying attention to experience, 39–41; productive and non-productive talking, 50–51; taking responsibility for, 43–47; talking about experience, 48–51; by Trying Harder, 38–39. *See also* relationships

emotions, positive and negative, 42

examples: Not Trying So Hard, 12, 17–21, 27, 31–33, 37–39, 44–45, 82, 109–10, 113–16; Trying

ABOUT THE AUTHOR

Avrum Geurin Weiss is a therapist, author, and teacher who has been interested in the process of change in people and organizations for over thirty years. He is the director of the Pine River Psychotherapy Training Institute and holds an adjunct faculty position in the Department of Psychology at Georgia State University. Avrum is the proud father of two grown children.

Connect with Avrum on Facebook (facebook.com/changehappens1) and follow him on Twitter (@changehappens1)